D0292163

A TREASURY OF THOUGHTS ON JEWISH PRAYER

BOOKS BY RABBI SIDNEY GREENBERG

Inspirational Essays:

Adding Life to Our Years
Finding Ourselves
Hidden Hungers
Say Yes to Life

Anthologies:

A Treasury of Comfort
The Bar Mitzvah Companion (Co-Editor)
Light from Jewish Lamps
A Treasury of the Art of Living
Teaching and Preaching: High Holiday Bible Themes
Volume I: Rosh Hashanah
Volume II: Yom Kippur

Youth Prayer Books:

Siddurenu (Co-Editor)
High Holiday Services for Children
Sabbath and Festival Services for Children
A Contemporary High Holiday Service (Co-Editor)
The New Model Seder (Co-Editor)
Junior Contemporary Prayer Book for the High Holidays (Co-Editor)

Prayer Books:

Contemporary Prayers and Readings for the High Holidays, Sabbaths, and Special Occasions
Likrat Shabbat: Worship, Study, and Song for Sabbath and Festival Evenings (Co-Editor)
The New Mahzor for Rosh Hashanah and Yom Kippur (Co-Editor)
A Minyan for Comfort

10 9 8 7 6 5 4 3 2

Library of Congress Cataloging-in-Publication Data

A treasury of thoughts on Jewish prayer / edited by Rabbi
Sidney Greenberg
p. cm.
ISBN 0-87668-865-2
1. Prayer—Judaism. 2. Jewish meditations. I. Greenberg.
Sidney, 1917– .
BM669.T46 1989
296.7'2—dc20 89-31455
CIP

Manufactured in the United States of America. Jason Aronson Inc. offers books and cassettes. For information and catalog write to Jason Aronson Inc., 230 Livingston Street, Northvale, New Jersey 07647.

A TREASURY OF THOUGHTS ON JEWISH PRAYER

Rabbi Sidney Greenberg

JASON ARONSON INC.
Northvale, New Jersey
London

LOVINGLY DEDICATED TO
HILDA
IN PARTIAL COMPENSATION FOR THE TIME
I STOLE FROM HER TO WORK ON THIS BOOK

CONTENTS

LIST OF ILLUSTRATIONS

LIST OF ILLUSTRATIONS

Page 1 — [illegible]

Page 30 — [illegible]

Page 73 — [illegible]

Page 97 — [illegible]

Page 124 — [illegible]

Page 137 — [illegible]

Page 165 — [illegible]

Page 189 — [illegible]

Page 231 — [illegible]

FOREWORD

American Jews don't know how to pray. They know how to attend synagogue services. They know how to rise when asked to, and how to resume their seats, and they know how to join in a responsive reading. They know how to listen to a sermon, how to join a discussion, and how to participate in the *kiddush* following services. But they don't know how to talk to God in prayer.

Part of the reason for this may be that today's Jews are not sure what they believe about God: Does He exist? Does He hear and answer prayer? Part of the reason may be that, when we read the siddur, we are not sure we believe what the prayers seem to be saying. And a big part of the reason may be that we are not sure exactly what it means to pray. We have come to think of prayer as asking God to give us something or to do something for us, and experience has taught us that we seldom get what we pray for.

I am told that the Eskimos have some two dozen words for "snow," because snow is a very important part of their environment. If prayer were an important part of our spiritual environment, we would probably have many words for it. Instead, we stretch the one word "prayer" to cover such different religious experiences as attending a public service and reading from a book, hoping for a favorable outcome to an operation—even as we realize that the result is in our hands—and gasping with delight at the beauty of the world when we wake up after a snowfall.

If we understood what it means to pray, if we understood why prayer has been an indispensable part of Jewish life for thousands of years, what would we gain? From public prayer we would gain the experience of overcoming our loneliness and becoming part of a congregation. From the concept of the *minyan*, we would learn that we are changed by being in the company of others. You are a different person in a group than you are when you are alone, and you are a different person in one group than you are in another. Alone, you may find it difficult to pray. In a room full of praying Jews, you too become a praying Jew (and amazingly, you have the power to help other people become praying Jews as well).

From the Torah service, we learn the holiness of study. Prayer happens not only when we speak to God, but when we put ourselves into a situation where we can hear God speaking to us. If the modern, college-educated Jew finds it easier to approach God through study than through performing rituals, we offer him or her a tradition that has always exalted study as one of the ways of finding and serving God, a tradition that sets the study of Torah at the heart of the *Shabbat* morning service.

From the liturgy, from the pages of the prayer book, we learn to be grateful. Jewish prayer does not say, "Give me . . . because I want it or need it." It says, "Thank you for all that I already have, too much of which I take for granted." The first page of the siddur will remind a Jew to be grateful for the fact that his mind works, his eyes, arms, legs work, he has clothes to wear and activities to look forward to as he begins a new day.

From personal prayer, we learn that we are not alone even when we feel most alone. When we are frightened of the future, when we are uncertain of our own ability to do something we know is right, prayer is our way of inviting God to come into our lives and help us. He may not make our path smooth and free of obstacles, but He will give us the grace to walk that path, however rocky, and He will give us the will to get up and continue, even when we stumble and fall.

There are a lot of things we today are able to do better than our ancestors ever could do. But they knew how to pray. When life was difficult, they knew how to turn to God for strength. When life was good to them, they knew how to celebrate and how to give their joyousness a cosmic dimension. Their prayers connected them to God and to their neighbors, and they never had to feel that they were alone. I can think of nothing we can do today that would help us enrich and deepen our lives more than recapturing the wisdom of generations past, by learning how to pray.

I don't know if a book can teach people to pray. But I do believe that in a book, especially in a book as rich and varied as this one, we can meet the souls of people who understood what it meant to pray. We can learn what praying meant to them, how it nourished their souls and why they would not have wanted to face life without that rich resource. And when we have met them, and listened to them, perhaps we too will be more ready to introduce our souls to the world of prayer.

Harold S. Kushner

INTRODUCTION

Solomon Schechter once drew a vital distinction between the two great classics of the Jewish faith. The Bible, he said, is the record of God's revelation to Israel; the siddur, the Jewish prayer book, is the record of Israel's self-revelation to God. In this crisp observation, Schechter gave to the prayer book its richly merited place of central significance in the spiritual life of the Jewish people throughout its history.

Dr. Henry Slonimsky, the renowned Bible scholar, went even further. He called the prayer book "the most important single Jewish book, a more personal expression, a closer record of Jewish sufferings, Jewish needs, Jewish hopes and aspirations than the Bible itself."

The recent proliferation of new editions of the prayer book by every branch of American Judaism bears witness to the enduring role that prayer plays in the spiritual life of the Jew. This phenomenon also indicates a widespread recognition that the prayer book must continue to meet the intellectual and emotional needs of our generation, and it must in our time, as in ages past, reflect the realities of contemporary life.

Precisely because prayer, like the Torah, "is the heritage of the house of Jacob"—the common concern and activity of every branch of American Judaism—it is to be expected that there will be diverse approaches to prayer and varying understandings of such questions as why we pray and what prayer accomplishes. Indeed, in each of the nine chapters of this anthology there will be reflected significant differences of opinion among the many people who are brought together between the covers of this book. Moreover, this divergence of thought will be found not only among the modern writers but also among the sages of the Talmud and the Midrash, as well as among the medieval Jewish philosophers and teachers.

This is not to imply that there are invariably differences among the various teachers and authors quoted in any chapter. Frequently the writers complement one another and fortify each other's observations with their own thoughts and insights. Prayer is like a resplendent jewel that casts a different radiance in accordance with the angle that the light falls upon it.

True to the function of the anthologist, the editor has made every effort to avoid weighting the selections in favor of his own intellectual and spiritual bias. He has tried to maintain a vigorous neutrality in his choice of passages, requiring of them only that they meet two basic criteria—Jewish authenticity and felicity of expression. Where these conditions were satisfied, any passage could gain admission, even where it did not agree with another passage in the book or with the editor's personal perspective. The editor took refuge behind the talmudic dictum that explicitly endorsed the recording and transmission of contradictory opinions: "These and these are the words of the living God."

But let us not dwell too much on the differences among the authors, because what unites them is by far more significant than what divides them. The areas of shared values and common concerns dominate, and the combined impact of their respective teachings can only serve to strengthen the impulse to worship and to validate prayer as one of the noblest and most sacred of all human endeavors.

This anthology was prepared in the fervent hope that it will promote a deeper understanding of the history of Jewish prayer, its rationale, its many-faceted capacity for deepening and enriching our lives. One of the authors we have included here is Robert Gordis, who delineated the extravagant rewards that prayer can confer.

"When men succeed in mastering the full art of prayer, they will have gained an inestimable resource for living with courage, insight, and joy. In the dark hours of trial and suffering that are inescapable in the human situation, prayer helps men to face life without fear or bitterness . . . in the days of well being and prosperity . . . the practice of prayer gives them . . . the capacity to see the Maker behind the made. . . . With the deepened sense of thanksgiving one's joy in life grows, as one experiences each day the miracle of creation. In essence, all man's prayers are an echo of the youthful Jacob at Beth-El: 'Indeed, God is in this place and I did not know it.'"

Abraham Isaac Kook put the matter in a single sentence: "Prayer is for us, as for all the world, an absolute necessity, and the purest of all joys."

1 WHAT IS PRAYER?

Prayer—The Heart of Significant Living

Prayer is at the heart not only of great religion, but of significant living. Without prayer we cannot scale the heights of compassion, or attain the peaks of love of our fellowman of which we are capable. Prayer has been an enduring and universal phenomenon of human life, not because a priesthood ordained it, nor because tradition hallowed it, but because man is ever seeking to probe into his own depths and bring to light his hidden yearnings. . . .

Prayer requires no consecrated edifice and no appointed hour. Indeed, it needs no words. Prayer is a step on which we rise from the self we are to the self we wish to be. Prayer affirms the hope that no reality can crush; the aspiration that can never acknowledge defeat. . . .

Prayer reveals truths about ourselves and the world that neither scalpel nor microscope can uncover. But prayer, to be a vital and transforming force in our life, cannot be an occasional mood, a moment's thought, a passing response, or a fugitive insight. It must be given permanence in our normal outlook and in our habitual behavior. Its rewards will be great, for it will not only ring us about with large horizons but will evoke from us the greatness to live in their presence. Wherever we go, we shall carry a Sanctuary with us. . . .

Prayer is not an escape from duty. It is no substitute for the deed. Prayer seeks the power to do wisely, to act generously, to live helpfully. It helps to re-enforce the act rather than to replace it. . . .

Prayer is the search for silence midst noise. Life is so filled with tumult that we do not hear ourselves. Failing to hear the voice of our spirit, can we hear the voice of God? . . .

There are those who are fearful to be alone with themselves. They run with the crowd not out of love for others but out of fear to remain alone with themselves, terrified lest they hear the voice of their own spirit, or fearful of remaining alone with their own void. . . .

Prayer takes us beyond the self. Joining our little self to the selfhood of humanity, it gives our wishes the freedom to grow large and broad and inclusive. Our prayers are answered not when we are given what we ask, but when we are challenged to be what we can be.

Morris Adler
The National Jewish Monthly

What It Means to Pray

Prayer, our Rabbis taught, is the Service of the Heart. Nothing is further from the truth than the widespread notion that to pray is synonymous with to beg, to request, or to supplicate.

To be sure, to pray means to call upon God to help us. But we need Him not only when we are physically in danger. We need Him also when we are spiritually in danger.

To pray means to seek God's help, "to keep our tongue from evil," "to purify our hearts," "to put into our hearts to understand, to learn and to fulfill in love, the words of the Torah," and thus to keep us unswervingly loyal to truth, goodness, and beauty.

To pray is to feel and to give expression to a deep sense of gratitude.

No intelligent, healthy, normal human being should take for granted, or accept without conscious, grateful acknowledgment the innumerable blessings which God in His infinite love bestows upon him daily—the blessings of parents and loved ones, of friends and country, of health and understanding.

To pray is to express renewed allegiance to the moral and ethical principles which we accept as the guides of our personal lives, and which we recognize as the indispensable foundation stones for a decent human society.

To pray is to meditate on events of the past which testify to God's guiding spirit in the affairs of men, and which give us courage to fight for justice and freedom, and to look confidently and hopefully to the future.

To pray is to experience the reality of God, to feel the purity and exaltation that comes from being near Him, and to give to our souls that serenity and peace which neither worldly success nor worldly failure, which neither the love of life, nor the fear of death, can disturb.

Simon Greenberg
Sabbath and Festival Prayer Book

Prayer Engages Mind and Heart

The rabbis defined prayer as "the service of the heart." This does not imply that the rabbis identified prayer with emotionalism, for prayer is equally rooted in man's convictions concerning God's reality. The prayers of the synagogue contain not only outpourings of the heart but also many affirmations of the nature of God, His relationship with Israel, His concern for every human being, and man's duty to live in accordance with God's revealed will. Prayer thus presupposes convictions of the mind even as it engages the emotions of the heart.

Abraham Millgram
Jewish Worship

When Prayer Is Divine Service of the Heart

When a man, overwhelmed by the impact of a specific experience, seeks the nearness of God or bursts forth in halleluyah or bows down in gratitude, it is prayer but not service of God yet; it is a human response to a potent stimulus. But when he prays without the stimulus of a specific occasion, acknowledging that man is always dependent on God, that independently of all personal experience God is always to be praised and to be thanked, then—and only then—is prayer divine service of the heart.

Eliezer Berkovits
Judaism

All Things Pray

It is not you alone, or we, or those others who pray; all things pray, all things pour forth their souls. The heavens pray, the earth prays, every creature and every living thing prays. In all life, there is longing. Creation is itself but a longing, a kind of prayer to the Almighty. What are the clouds, the rising and the setting of the sun, the soft radiance of the moon, and the gentleness of the night? What are the flashes of the human mind and the storms of the human heart? They are all prayers—the outpouring of boundless longing for God.

Micha Josef Berdyczewski
Tefillah Shebalev

Use and Misuse of Prayer

Sometimes prayer amounts to nothing but a piece of conventionality. Sometimes it retains vestiges of primitive magic, operating as a kind of incantation imagined to be efficacious. Many a prayer is but an act of dull dead conformity tinged with superstition. That is one of the possibilities. By contrast, prayer can also be the voice of one's loftiest ideals. It can dramatize one's noblest aspirations. It can express one's love and devotion toward others. It can articulate one's profoundest yearning for the wise, the blessed and the true.

Abraham Cronbach
CCAR Yearbook 1947

Why Should We Pray at All?

The smart question is why we should have to pray at all to a God who should know us and who therefore should supply our wants without our troubling Him.

Our theory of the correlation of God and man, whereby they mutually re-enforce each other in a mystic life-giving circle, growing together through each other's gift and enrichment, holds for religion as for all the major creative efforts of man—for music and poetry and the arts of beauty, as for the visions of justice and government and character and love. God is the source of inspiration, but man must do the work and give it back to

Him enriched—fashioned, articulated, built. "In Thy light we see light" is the simple literal truth: inspiration is from God. But it is we who must weave that light into a fabric and utterance. God hands a chalice to mankind which mankind must hand back to Him at the end of days, foaming with its own inner saps and juices, its own sweat and blood and wine, its own infinite experience. Not the alternative of Christian theology, God's grace or man's works, but the two together is the subtle and profound position of Jewish religious thinking. Thus Akiba, the greatest of the rabbis, tells us at the end of the Mishna tractate on Yom Kippur, as the consummating thought of that tractate, "Happy are you O Israel: before whom do you cleanse yourselves, and who cleanses you? Your Father which is in heaven." Not man alone, not God alone, but the two together confront a world which is mere material for being made divine.

Henry Slonimsky
Gates of Understanding

Prayer—A Home for the Soul

Prayer is not a stratagem for occasional use, a refuge to resort to now and then. It is rather like an established residence for the innermost self. All things have a home, the bird has a nest, the fox has a hole, the bee has a hive. A soul without prayer is a soul without a home. Weary, sobbing, the soul, after running through a world festered with aimlessness, falsehoods, and absurdities, seeks a moment in which to gather up its scattered life, in which to divest itself of enforced pretensions and camouflage, in which to simplify complexities, in which to call for help without being a coward. Such a home is prayer.

Abraham Joshua Heschel
Man Is Not Alone

To Make God Our Confidant

In its original form, prayer is not asking God for anything; it is not a request. It is a cry; an elementary outburst of woe, a spontaneous call in need; a hurt, a sorrow, given voice. It is the call of human helplessness directed to God. It is not asking, but coming with one's burden before God. It is like the child's running to the mother because it hurts. It is not the bandage that the child seeks instinctively but the nearness of the mother, to unburden his heart to the one of whose love he is certain. So the human being brings his sorrow before God: look, O God, what has been done to me, consider what has become of me. This is the essence of prayer. Only children can pray like this or—*Tsadikim*, the men of great faith who in the depth of their piety have gained a new child-like trust in God. Interpreting the words of the psalmist: "I pour out my complaint before Him, I declare before Him my trouble," the Midrash remarks: "Thus the men of faith declare their troubles before God." In all their simplicity, these few words, which seem to add nothing to the text, are among the deepest observations on the essence of prayer. To pour out one's heart before God means simply to tell God about one's troubles. To pray means to make God the confidant of one's sorrow and need. The asking and begging are natural enough, but they are of secondary importance. Decisive is the pouring out of the heart because one has to; the pouring out of the heart before God because He is the nearest, because He is the closest, because He is the natural confidant of the human soul. All asking is in reality self-seeking; whether we ask for bread or health, for the power to do good, or "the enjoyment of God," we are asking for ourselves, for the things that we desire. "Give, give!" is no prayer, no matter what we ask for. We may ask only if we pray, if we cry with the need of the creature; if the request comes without premeditation in the wake of the cry. Our asking may have the quality of prayer, if it issues from the act of intimacy, of having made God our confidant.

Eliezer Berkovits
Studies in Torah Judaism

People think that you pray to God, but that is not the case. Rather prayer itself is of the essence of Divinity.

Rabbi Pinchas of Kuretz
Menorah Ha-Tehorah

The Brazen Act

Prayer is a brazen act. For it is impossible to stand before God, blessed be He, but brazenly. Every man imagines—in one way or another—the greatness of the Creator: How then can one stand in prayer before Him? For prayer is a wonder; (its task is) chiefly the assault upon, and the despoiling of, the heavenly order. . . . Man comes wishing to despoil the order and do marvels. Therefore man must be shameless in prayer.

Nachman of Bratzlav
Likutay Etzot Ha-Shem

Prayer—A Supreme Chutzpah

Prayer, if we think about it carefully, is actually a supreme manifestation of impertinence, of *chutzpah*. But such is the unique Jewish stance towards God that, according to one view in the Talmud, "*Chutzpah*, even against God, is of avail." The underlying impertinence of prayer is the tacit assumption that man has but to open his mouth, and God will hear his prayer. Man does not deal in this fashion with his own human authorities. The ordinary citizen has little hope of ever communicating directly with the head of his government. At best, he will be heard by a subordinate official on some lower echelon of the administration. Yet man takes it for granted that he may have an audience with the Sovereign of the whole Universe, the Holy One, praised be He, at any time he chooses. That is the great daring, the *chutzpah* underlying the act of prayer.

Jakob J. Petuchowski
Dynamics and Doctrine

It is written, "Love the Lord your God, and serve Him with all your heart" (Deuteronomy 11:13).

What is the service of the heart? We say that it is prayer.

Taanit 2a

In Prayer We Shift the Center of Living

Prayer is our attachment to the utmost. Without God in sight, we are like the scattered rungs of a broken ladder. To pray is to become a ladder on which thoughts mount to God to join the movement toward Him which surges unnoticed throughout the entire universe. We do not step out of the world when we pray; we merely see the world in a different setting. The self is not the hub, but the spoke of the revolving wheel. In prayer we shift the center of living from self-consciousness to self-surrender. God is the center toward which all forces tend. He is the source, and we are the flowing of His force, the ebb and flow of His tides.

Abraham Joshua Heschel
Man's Quest for God

The Bridge of Prayer

Prayer is the bridge between man and God.

With the intellect one figures out what God *is* and also something of what He must be.

In intuition one experiences Him.

In revelation one receives testimony concerning Him, more or less definitive according to the credence given it.

In the good life one charts a course by His light.

In ritual one celebrates Him.

But only in prayer does one establish a soul to soul interchange with Him.

Prayer then consists in two elements: that a soul shall be oriented toward God; and that, whether with words or not, it shall address Him.

Milton Steinberg
Basic Judaism

Prayer Is a Bridge

Can prayer still be meaningful and relevant to the modern Jew? Prayer is the bridge between God and man, but it can also be the bridge between Jew and Jew. "*Vetaher libenu,*" and purify our hearts—these words are known to most Jews, if not from the prayer book, then as the text of a horah. Even at the time of the greatest estrangement between the chalutzim and the traditionalists, the chalutzim could still express in the language of dance what the pious Jews expressed in the language of prayer. From the Torah to *chalutziut*, there is a continuous stream of religious consciousness which has bound together all our habitations and generations. Prayer can create a unity of experience which transcends the boundaries of time and space and bridges the diversity of conviction.

Ernst Simon
Prayer: A Study in the History and Psychology of Religion

Human Agony Turned God-ward

Because it is only on account of the needfulness of our humanity that we may pray, there is no creaturely need out of which we dare not call God. Be it the body or the soul, the affliction of the individual or the group, of man or mankind, in prayer we tumble into the presence of God with our load. Thus, even prayers for vengeance, which at first glance rightly scandalize us, may be genuine prayers; and more so than the noblest literary exercises composed by philosophers in the peace of their study and in accordance with the ultimate principles of some ethical theory. A greater man of prayer than the prophet Jeremiah one can hardly conceive. Yet, he did supplicate in the words:

> But, O Lord of hosts, that triest the righteous,
> That seest the reins and the heart,
> Let me see Thy vengeance on them;
> For unto Thee have I revealed my cause.

Now, such a prayer, incorporated in a planned service in a synagogue that begins at 9:00 A. M., and has to be over by 11:00 A. M., one to which people get dressed up in their Sabbath-best fully conscious that it is doing what is only right and proper, such a prayer introduced at what we have come to call a divine service, would indeed be an abomination. But to compare our way of praying with that of a Jeremiah would be a sacrilege committed against the prophet.

Those words of Jeremiah are indeed terrible words, but prayer may be terrible and yet be prayer and, perhaps, even more prayer on account of the terror that breathes in it. Not what the prophet asks for makes his words prayer, but that they are the creaturely cry of a greatly afflicted soul of a man hunted and persecuted for going about the business of God, a mission moreover for which he has not asked but which—very much against his will—was imposed upon him by God. Those words are prayer because they were uttered by Jeremiah, the man whose life-experience was summed up when he poured out his heart:

Cursed be the day
Wherein I was born;
The day wherein my mother bore me,
Let it not be blessed.

Those words of the prophet are prayer because they are the elementary utterance of a life of "labor and sorrow" which made the prophet turn to the only one to whom he could turn with the exclamation at the end of which his cry for vengeance is found:

O Lord, Thou hast enticed me, and I was enticed,
Thou hast overcome me, and hast prevailed;
I am become a laughing-stock all the day,
Everyone mocketh me.
For as often as I speak, I cry out,
I cry: 'Violence and spoil';
Because the word of the Lord is made
A reproach unto me, and a derision all the day

All this is prayer because it is human agony turned God-ward.

Eliezer Berkovits
Studies in Torah Judaism: Prayer

To Pray We Must Believe We Can Grow

The rabbis of Eastern Europe, in the eighteenth century, taught, "The greatest evil is when you forget that you are the son of a king!" This was their way of saying that man will live optimistically and creatively only if he remembers, at all times, that he is wonderfully formed by a God who cares. In our highly urbanized and competitive society, it is easy for the individual to conclude that he is an insignificant speck in a swarming mass. The pages of Genesis would teach us otherwise. The text informs us that man is made in the "image of God." While contemporaries of the early Hebrews taught that the king was divine and that his subjects were a mere shadow of the king's being, the Hebrews taught that each man is made of the divine stuff itself!

Prayer is not possible unless one has a reasonable evaluation of his own importance. Those who belittle or hate themselves despair of ever leading meaningful lives and find it difficult to pray. To pray, you must believe yourself capable of change and growth towards the "image of the Divine." Looked at in this light, prayer is an exalted tool leading to the reawakening of the sense of one's own worthwhileness. It is a channel by which the individual river can link itself to the great ocean of life. It is a way of learning, a way of reaffirming the fact that we live in a kingdom greater than the kingdom of the individual. Prayer is a way to the tapping of a power greater than the individual believes he has. It is the process of becoming increasingly a part of the greater life in which we move and which flows through us at all times.

Herbert M. Baumgard
Judaism and Prayer

Prayer—A Complete Turning of The Heart to God

The focus of prayer is not the self. A man may spend hours meditating about himself, or be stirred by the deepest sympathy for his fellow man, and no prayer will come to pass. Prayer comes to pass in a complete turning of the heart toward God, toward His goodness and power. It is the momentary disregard of our personal concerns, the absence of self-centered thoughts, which constitute the art of prayer. Feeling becomes prayer in the moment in which we forget ourselves and become aware of God. When we analyze the consciousness of a supplicant, we discover that it is not concentrated upon his own interests, but on something beyond the self. The thought of personal need is absent, and the thought of divine grace alone is present in his mind. Thus, in beseeching Him for bread, there is *one* instant, at least, in which our mind is directed neither to our hunger nor to food, but to His mercy. This instant is prayer.

Abraham Joshua Heschel
Man's Quest for God

Prayer—A Natural Urge

Prayer is the manifestation of the natural urge in every human being to give expression to his innermost feelings. Primitive man stood in amazement as he scanned the wonderful and mysterious world around him. When he watched the sun burst forth in golden rays he felt an inner urge to express his emotions of awe and wonder. The waters cascading down the mountainside, a mighty river flowing without cease, the peals of thunder reverberating, the flashes of lightning piercing the sky, the multicolored flowers carpeting the landscape, the variety of foods and the diverse vegetation sustaining mankind—all these phenomena brought forth wonder, amazement, fear, reverence and thankfulness. To whom? Very early in history it must have been to the Creator, to God as man conceived God. The impelling force in man was to express in words his mental and emotional experiences to the Creator, to God. These expressions we call prayer.

Joshua Cohen
The Synagogue in Jewish Life

True prayer is a search for God, the answer is finding Him.

Israel I. Mattuck
Service of the Heart

Signposts

Prayers are signposts along the way, visible even in the fog, pointing in the right direction and reminding us what to remember.

Samuel H. Dresner
Prayer, Humility, and Compassion

Rabbi Yehudah says: Repentance does half, and prayer does all.

Leviticus Rabbah 10:5

The Very Essence of Prayer

Prayer is basically an awareness of man finding himself in the presence or and addressing himself to his Maker, and to pray has one connotation only: to stand before God. To be sure, this awareness has been objectified and crystallized in standardized, definitive texts whose recitation is obligatory. The total faith commitment tends always to transcend the frontiers of fleeting, amorphous subjectivity and to venture into the outside world of the well-formed, objective gesture. However, no matter how important this tendency on the part of the faith commitment is—and it is of enormous significance in the Halakhah which constantly demands from man that he translate his inner life into external facticity—it remains unalterably true that the very essence of prayer is the covenantal experience of being together with and talking to God and that the concrete performance such as the recitation of texts represents the technique of implementation of prayer and not prayer itself.

Joseph Soloveitchik
The Lonely Man of Faith

Prayer is the soul of man holding converse with the soul of the universe.

Israel Bettan
Studies in Jewish Preaching

Prayer—The Encounter between the I and the Great Thou

We may not be able to meet God in prayer. But prayer makes it possible for us to reach the meeting point between God and man, the moment—that point in time—when the I encounters the great Thou. We cannot reach more, but this point we can reach. And in the rare moments in which we are able to reach this meeting point, we reach beyond ourselves.

Ernst Simon
Tradition and Contemporary Experience

Prayer Points to the Ultimate Goal of Man's Existence

To pray is to turn to God as our creator whom we praise and thank. To pray is to stand before Him as our judge to whom we address our supplications. To pray is to acknowledge Him as the giver of Torah which we are to study. Ultimately, however, every Jewish prayer ends with the *Aleynu* in which we turn to Him as the God of the future which will see mankind's redemption. Thus, prayer is a gate to our living past. As we probe its enduring meaning, it can become a source of power that points to the ultimate goal of man's existence.

Ernst Simon
Tradition and Contemporary Experience

The Multiplicity of the Forms of Prayer

Prayer appears in history in an astonishing multiplicity of forms; as the calm collectedness of a devout individual soul, and as the ceremonial liturgy of a great congregation; as an original creation of a religious genius, and as an imitation on the part of a simple, average religious person; as the spontaneous expression of upspringing religious experiences, and as the mechanical recitation of an incomprehensible formula; as bliss and ecstasy of heart, and as painful fulfillment of the law; as the involuntary discharge of an overwhelming emotion, and as the voluntary concentration on a religious object; as loud shouting and crying, and as still, silent absorption; as artistic poetry, and as stammering speech; as the flight of the spirit to the supreme Light, and as a cry out of the deep distress of the heart; as joyous thanksgiving and ecstatic praise, and as humble supplication for forgiveness and compassion; as a childlike entreaty for life, health, and happiness, and as an earnest desire for power in the moral struggle for existence; as a simple petition for daily bread, and as an all-consuming yearning for God Himself; as a selfish wish, and as unselfish solicitude for a brother; as wild cursing and vengeful thirst, and as heroic intercession for personal enemies and persecutors; as a stormy clamor and demand, and as joyful renunciation and holy serenity; as a desire to change God's will and make it chime with our petty wishes, and as a self-forgetting vision of and surrender to the Highest Good; as the timid entreaty of the sinner before a stern judge, and as the trustful talk of a child with a kind father; as swelling phrases of politeness and flattery before an unapproachable King, and as a free outpouring in the presence of a Friend who cares.

Max Heiler
Studies in Torah Judaism: Prayer

Prayer is the most intensely personal expression of the human soul.

Abraham A. Neuman
Landmarks and Goals

When Man Recognizes that He Stands in the Presence of God

Whatever else prayer may be, it is minimally *what a man does when he recognizes that he stands in the presence of God.* This is the basic truth about prayer. I am not referring now to study groups in which we speculate and philosophize about God; nor do I have in mind the conversations with our children in which we struggle to demonstrate God's existence to them. I mean the immediately experienced reality of our own position in the presence of God. Either we know this reality or we do not. And what I am saying is that prayer is what a man does when he knows it.

Dudley Weinberg
The Efficacy of Prayer

Surrendering to the Stillness that Surrounds Us

Prayer is a surrendering to the stillness that surrounds us, a withdrawal from the marketplace, the honking of horns, the television set, the innumerable diversions and attractions which modern living thrusts upon us, and a yielding to the quiet that is everywhere. For there is another world about and within us which we neither see nor touch, a world which is as real as the flowers we smell or the ground we walk upon, as the mountains we behold or the rock we lean against. There is One who at all times and in all places speaks to us with love and guidance and concern; but He speaks in a tone barely audible and we must clear away the din of daily living and open our ears to hear Him.

Samuel H. Dresner
Prayer, Humility, and Compassion

Every thought of God is prayer. Holy, true and honest purposes are prayer. Earnest thought, search without vanity is prayer.

Rachel Levin Varnhagen
Briefe

Prayer Opens a Man's Eyes

It is the attitude of the man at prayer which is decisive. The pious man believes that God hears his prayers and that He can and will answer them *"if it seemeth good in His eyes"* to do so. God cannot be thought of as a sort of clerk in heaven who simply registers our requests and automatically grants them. Such a view is surely blasphemous. The decision must be left to Him. Many things which may seem good and proper to us may yet have deficiencies which are hidden from our puny comprehension but which are clear to the comprehensive vision of the All-Knowing God. The fly which crawls over a canvas and finds its progress impeded by a blob of paint is completely unaware of the importance of this obstacle from the larger point of view. So it may be with seeming hardships and obstacles in the path of man. The verse of the Psalmist: "The Lord is nigh unto all who call unto Him, to all who call upon Him *in truth,"* has been interpreted to refer to those who continue to trust in Him and His goodness even when their own specific wishes are not fulfilled. And the teaching of the Mishnah (Avot 2), "Do not make thy prayer *Keva*, but supplication and prayer"—has been given various interpretations in the Talmud (Berachot 29b), one of which explains its meaning to be:

> Do not make thy prayer *keva*— a fixed claim or demand which you insist must be fulfilled—but only a supplication for mercy and grace which may or may not be acceded to.

In fact, merely seeking the satisfaction and gratification of one's own desires, in a purely selfish way, would be a form of self-worship. But the man who asks even for ordinary earthly material benefits like health, sustenance, riches, can come to regard these very human goals as sanctified through the realization that they, too, emanate from God. The efficacy of prayer, in short, is to be understood not only in terms of having one's petitions granted, but in its effectiveness as an influence on human living and striving and a means of lifting man's heart to the service of God.

And finally, prayer opens a man's eyes and makes him conscious of the constant answer which God gives to the world in renewing it in all its glory from day to day. Judaism teaches us to see in this the greatest and most constantly recurring of miracles in answer to the needs of mortal creatures. "For He renews, in His goodness, constantly, every day, the works of Creation."

Bernard M. Casper
Talks on Jewish Prayer

Prayer—A Vehicle through Which Man and God Strengthen Each Other

Judaism has taught that not only do men give strength to each other, but righteous men help to give God strength. The mass slaughter of millions of Jews in World War II, like other human catastrophies, underscores the fact that the inhumanity of man to man is a betrayal of God. God must have human agents to administer laws rooted in His nature. Righteous men project His power into the world. He must have mediators and intercessors as Moses and Jeremiah classically demonstrated. This viewpoint has been ably presented by my revered teacher, Dr. Henry Slonimsky, who has written, "They (i.e., man and God) become allies in the most redoubtable of all struggles and for the greatest of all stakes. . . . But in a very real sense, the fate of God and of the future rests on the heroism of man, on what he elects to do, for he is . . . the focus of decision."

The Maggid of Zlotchov expounded on the verse, "Ye shall be holy: for I, the Lord, your God, am holy." He taught, "This is what is meant: *'My holiness,' which is the world, depends upon your holiness.* As you sanctify My name below, so it is sanctified in the heights of Heaven. For it is written: *'Give ye strength unto God.'* "

Prayer, then, is not merely a one-way street. It is a vehicle through which man and God strengthen each other, as men and God, together, sanctify the world by serving each other. God has His work, as witness the endless power which He pipes into the universe, but there are certain tasks reserved for man, which man alone can do and must do in moving the mutual cause forward. Dr. Slonimsky has written, "God hands a chalice to mankind which mankind must hand back to Him at the end of days, foaming with its own inner saps and juices, its own sweat and blood and wine, its own infinite experience."

"Religion," wrote Montague, "is a momentous possibility, the possibility namely that what is highest in spirit is also deepest in nature—that there is something at the heart of nature, something akin to us, a conserver and increaser of values . . . that the things that matter most are not at the mercy of the things that matter least." Judaism suggests that this "something at the heart of nature" is concerned with us as individuals and that prayer is a yearning ". . . which God Himself puts into our hearts to give back to Him enriched by our fervor, our power."

"To act out of love," wrote Slonimsky, "and to be willing to bear the suffering which the good and true man must inevitably bear in a world like ours, in a world which is only partly divine and which must be won for God through the efforts of man—that is the deepest utterance of the rabbis and the culminating idea of Jewish religiosity and of Jewish prayer."

Not God alone. Not man alone. But God and man together, interacting and tied together, in a never-ending process of prayer and work (*avodah*).

Herbert M. Baumgard
Judaism and Prayer

Prayer in Israel teaches man to overcome bitterness and self-pity; to think not of what the world owes him, but what he owes the world and God.

Solomon B. Freehof
The Small Sanctuary

What Prayer Can and Cannot Do

Prayer cannot mend a broken bridge, rebuild a ruined city, or bring water to parched fields.

Prayer can mend a broken heart, lift up a discouraged soul, and strengthen a weakened will.

Ferdinand M. Isserman
Sermons and Addresses

The Power to Transform Life

The real value of prayer lies in its power to transform a man's life. When sincerely and regularly practiced—whether spoken or unspoken—it has the effect of lifting one out of the slough of despair and the mire of fear. It can perform a veritable miracle in our lives by bringing us nearer to God.

Julius Mark
The Message of Israel

Beloved Is Prayer

Beloved is prayer before the Holy One, Blessed be He, more than a hundred good deeds and more than all the sacrifices.

Berachot 32a

Prayer Is Joyous Recognition

Prayer is awareness not only of God but of oneself as well. God is what He is and we are what we are whether we recognize and welcome it or not. Prayer is a joyous recognition and deliberate thankful acceptance of what we are.

Dudley Weinberg
The Efficacy of Prayer

Prayer Has Changed Lives

Is it superstition to believe that God hears prayer and answers us? Yes, if we believe that whenever we say something or do something magical then God must jump to our command. But, it is not superstitious to hope that, if we call, He will hear. What would stop Him from hearing us? Why should He not hear? Magic tries to accomplish something against God. Prayer tries to tell Him something, leaving it to Him to do what He wishes. Magic accomplishes something or tries to. Prayer is itself accomplishment.

To be heard by God is to be forgiven of our errors and changed into better people. Prayer does not insure that we get what we want, but only what God wants. It cannot cure cancer or win races, but it can change lives. It has.

Arnold Wolf
Challenge to Confirmands

A Source of Strength and Comfort

If there were not something in the universe that draws us, as the moon draws the sea, man's high aspirations would have no meaning. Tides prove the moon is there, even though clouds may cover it. . . . Aspiration is an expression of something deeper than intellect; a profound certainty that beyond man's body and beyond his mind there is a spiritual content in the universe with which his own spirit can from time to time communicate and from which he can draw strength and comfort . . . this sense of Presence, this central, orienting core of things, is what we mean by God.

Edmond Sinnot
The Bridge of Life

The Spirit within Reaching Out

We are formed by the same forces—chemical, physical, and spiritual—which hold the stars in their orbit, thrust up the mountains, scoop out the seas, bring the rose to bloom, teach the hawk to fly, the horse to neigh. "If I climb up unto the heavens, behold Thou art there, and, if I go to the ends of the earth, behold Thou art there" (Psalm 139:8).

Prayer is not the lonely cry of a "tailless monkey playing ape to his dreams," nor a shout into an empty void answered only by its own echo. Prayer is the spirit within us reaching out to the Spirit of the universe, and prayer is that Spirit responding to us.

Robert I. Kahn
Prayer and Its Expression

Prayer—Nourishment of the Soul

The hour of worship is both the core and the mature fruit of one's time, while all other hours are like the channels leading to it . . . they stand in the same relation to the soul as food to the body. Prayer is to the soul what nourishment is to the body, and the blessing one derives from prayer lasts until it is time to pray again, just as the strength derived from the midday meal lasts till the evening meal.

Yehuda Halevi
Kuzari

2 THE REASONS WE PRAY

Through Prayer Man Lifts Up All Creation

Every plant and bush, every grain of sand and clod of earth, everything in which life is revealed or hidden, the smallest and the biggest in creation—all longs and yearns and reaches out toward its celestial source. And at every moment, all these cravings are gathered up and absorbed by man, who is himself lifted up by the longing for holiness within him. It is during prayer that all these pent-up desires and yearnings are released. Through his prayer man unites in himself all being, and lifts all creation up to the fountainhead of blessing and life.

Abraham Isaac Kook
Jewish Thought

Discovering Our Own Hidden Treasures

The ultimate purpose of Torah study is not merely to inform but to lead to the inner development of the individual. This is a primary viewpoint of Judaism. *The purpose of all learning and praying is the development of human beings who are able to relate together on the higher levels of love and understanding, who are able to construct and participate in the good society on this earth.* In the end, what is sought is the transformation of the individual and society.

Bachya, writing on the purpose of meditation and study, contended, "My aim is rather to bring to light the root principles of our religion that are deeply fixed in the unsophisticated intellect—those pivot principles of our Torah which are *latent in our souls.* Once we rouse our minds to meditate on them, their truth becomes clear to us *inwardly* and their bright rays will even be manifest to us externally. The following is an apt analogy. An astrologer went to a friend's courtyard, and divined that it contained a hidden treasure. He searched for it, and found a mass of silver that had turned black and had lost its lustre because of the rust with which it had become encrusted. He took some of the metal, scoured it with salt and vinegar, washed and polished it, till it had recovered its original lustre, beauty and brightness. The owner then gave orders that the rest of the treasure should be similarly treated. I wish to do the same with the hidden treasures of the heart; namely, to bring them to light and to exhibit their shining excellence so that anyone who desires to draw near to God and cling to Him may do likewise." According to Bachya, the ultimate purpose of study is to lead the student to inward reflection to discover his own hidden treasures. When study inspires this kind of reflection, it partakes of the nature of prayer, for it inspires us to reach for the divine within ourselves.

We must keep in mind, then, that where we seek the "hidden treasures" in Jewish lore, our ultimate purpose is to reveal the hidden treasures within ourselves. We are seeking to develop that within ourselves which is real but latent. To do this, we may have to work at scouring and washing and polishing, but it can be done, and must be done, if we are to attain to our higher potential.

Herbert M. Baumgard
Judaism and Prayer

All the various component parts of the Hebrew worship subserve this great purpose, the bringing of man into communication with God.

Samson Raphael Hirsch
Nineteen Letters

The Double Effect of Prayer

Self-expression before God in prayer has thus a double effect: It strengthens faith in God's love and kindness, as well as His all-wise and all-bountiful prescience. But it also chastens the desires and feelings of man, teaching him to banish from his heart all thoughts of self-seeking and sin, and to raise himself toward the purity and the freedom of the divine will and demand.

Kaufmann Kohler
Jewish Theology

To Be Touched by Life Again

No one escapes the anguish of existence, but for some, this anguish can be borne because of their belief.

In *The Human Season*, by Edward Lewis Wallant, a Jew who has lost his dearly beloved wife turns against God with blasphemy and rejection. He isolates himself from his family and from his world. Then one day, in the midst of his rage against God, he touches a live wire in his home.

Suddenly ferocious life snaked up his arm and reached for his heart. He gave a loud cry as the electricity shot through him. He felt himself thrown, as though by a gigantic hand, down to the floor. Stunned, he lay there. He didn't know if he could move, refused to try.

In the emptiness he began to cry, a simple, childlike weeping. Then because there was nothing else, because his thoughts and his grievances were amputated for the moment, and he was left only with some of the old reflexes of the spirit, he began to moan:

Baruch atah Adonai . . . God in Heaven . . . Mary, Mary, my wife . . . forgive me. . . . *V'yiskadash* . . . *Gott im Himmel* . . . forgive me. . . .

He wished with all his heart not to die there on the living room floor, so senselessly, with no chance to make a little peace with himself.

In a mingling of the languages he had spoken in his life, English, Russian, Yiddish, he prayed without realizing he prayed, begged with no memory of pride, to come out of that living death he had made for himself, to be touched by life again.

David Polish
The Need to Pray

We Cannot Help Praying

Prayer is a universal phenomenon in the soul-life of man. It is the soul's reaction to the terrors and joys, the uncertainties and dreams of life. "The reason why we pray," says William James, "is simply that we cannot help praying." It is an instinct that springs eternally from man's unquenchable faith in a living God, almighty and merciful, Who heareth prayer, and answereth those who call upon Him in truth; and it ranges from half-articulate petition for help in distress to highest adoration, from confession of sin to jubilant expression of joyful fellowship with God, from thanksgiving to the solemn resolve to do His will as if it were our will. Prayer is a Jacob's ladder joining earth to heaven; and, as nothing else, wakens in the children of men the sense of kinship with their Father on high. It is "an ascent of the mind to God"; and, in ecstasies of devotion, man is raised above all earthly cares and fears. The Jewish mystics compare the action of prayer upon the human spirit to that of the flame on the coal. "As the flame clothes the black, sooty clod in a garment of fire, and releases the heat imprisoned therein, even so does prayer clothe a man in a garment of holiness, evoke the light and fire implanted within him by his Maker, illumine his whole being, and unite the Lower and the Higher World" (Zohar).

Joseph H. Hertz
Daily Prayer Book

The Various Types of Prayers

Since man turns to God in many moods and designs, prayers are equally numerous and diverse as to temper and purpose. Certain types, however, recur with high frequency, no doubt because they articulate common and elemental emotions.

Of these the most notable are:

The prayer of *contemplation,* in which man meditates on God and His will;

The prayer of *adoration*, in which the greatness and mystery of God are considered;

The prayer of *thanksgiving,* in which, having experienced God's goodness, man puts into words his gratitude and indebtedness;

The prayer of *affirmation*, which crystallizes the faith of the believer and his aspirations;

The prayer of *resignation*, in which, his own devices and strength exhausted, man casts his burdens on the Lord;

The prayer of *penitence,* wherein the guilty conscience confesses his guilt and appeals for purification from it;

The prayer of *protest,* the pouring forth of human indignation against the injustices of the world and the voiced demand that they be set right;

The prayer of *quest*, in which, lost and confused, man gropes for light and direction, sometimes for the very God to whom he addresses his supplications;

The prayer of *petition*, in which the heart's desires are asked for, whether they be things physical or spiritual, whether for self or for others.

Of these major categories of prayer, examples can be found almost anywhere in life and letters but with extraordinary wealth and profusion in Scripture—the Book of Psalms in particular—in rabbinic literature, and especially in the established Jewish prayer books. If the reader will turn to these source texts, he will find in them fascinating instances of the shapes and powers of this tool of the spirit.

Milton Steinberg
Basic Judaism

We Pray to Him Because He Knows All

How long should a prayer be? There are differences of opinion on this between the teachers of the Talmud, as there may well be. However, the opinion of Rabbi Yochanan has become the accepted Halaka, according to which, "Would that man prayed all day." Indeed, who would wish to limit the outpourings of an afflicted soul! Shall we say to a man: Don't bother the Almighty; He is perfectly well informed about your plight! One might as well upbraid a child, seeking the comforting arms of the mother, since she knows all about the child's troubles and need not be informed. We pray because we have to pour out our hearts to the One who knows all. Yes, we do it, *because* He knows all and understands all. If he were not omniscient, we would not come before Him so free of all shyness in the needfulness of our nature.

Eliezer Berkovits
Studies in Torah Judaism: Prayer

Prayer—A Natural Bridge between Ultimate Reality and Myself

Is there room in a naturalistic and rationalistic theology for prayer? Will it help toward an answer if I attest that here is one naturalistic, rationalistic, religious Jew who prays every day of his life? Who prays, moreover, out of deep conviction that his prayers can have major consequences. Who believes that within the natural order of things there is something in the universe which is responsive to his prayers.

I resort to analogy once more, aware of the fact that all analogies are imperfect. The main difficulty with this one is that it makes God seem impossibly mechanical and cold. Yet perhaps it will nonetheless clarify what prayer can mean to a naturalist. At various locations in my home, as in yours, there are faucets. Each of these is the terminal point of a pipe, which leads back to a water main, which in turn is connected to a pumping station. When I in my thirst seek a drink of water, does the engineer in that pumping station respond to my need? Not in the sense that I petition him for water and he, on the basis of my past conduct or his affection for me, decides to grant my request. Not even in the sense that he is directly aware at that moment of my thirst. But in a larger and more significant way, the engineer does respond to my need: in fact, he has responded to it even before I myself was aware of it. He has created a system which makes it possible for my need to be met provided (a) I understand the nature of the system, and (b) I understand the nature of myself and my relationship to the system, and (c) I assume my share of responsibility to activate the system. Lacking these three requisites, I can stand before the faucet all day long, piteously begging for water, and my thirst will not be slaked.

With all its admitted imperfections, this comes close to expressing a naturalistic concept of prayer. It holds that God is a spiritual Force or Power—throughout the universe and in each of us—which makes it possible for us to rise above our ordinary understandings and accomplishments. God is there, whether we pray or not. God performs His necessary work in sustaining and operating the universe, whether we pray or not. Our words of worship in no way alter God or change His course of conduct. They can, however, alter us. They can make us aware of spiritual potential of which we are otherwise oblivious. And by helping us—if you will forgive the commercial terminology—by helping us to capitalize on that potential, they can change our lives immeasurably. In short, prayer too can be understood as a natural phenomenon, as a meaningful relationship between nature and the individual, as a natural bridge between Ultimate Reality and myself.

Roland B. Gittelsohn
Gates of Understanding

To Return the Words to Their Source

The purpose of all prayer is to uplift the words,
to return them to their source above.
The world was created
by the downward flow of letters:
The task of man is to form those letters into words
and take them back to God.
If you come to know this dual process,
your prayer may be joined
to the constant flow of Creation—
word to word, voice to voice,
breath to breath, thought to thought.

The words fly upward and come before Him.
As God turns to look at the ascending word,
life flows through all the worlds
and prayer receives its answer.
All this happens in an instant
and all this happens continually;
Time has no meaning in the sight of God.
The divine spring is ever-flowing;
one who is ready can make himself into a channel
to receive the waters from above.

Likkutim Yekarim 10a
Arthur Green
Barry Holtz
Your Word Is Fire

In Worship We Are Freed from the Pressure of Life

When we come together for worship, we free ourselves from a host of activities, a multitude of concerns with which, at other times, we are preoccupied. We stand aside from all that makes up our business or professional life. We withdraw ourselves from family cares. We escape from daily routine and, in some measure, from daily worries.

Normally, we are compelled to pass from one task to another in quick succession; one duty is completed only to be followed immediately by the next; a difficulty surmounted, a problem solved is replaced with such rapidity by further worries and by other cares that we have no choice, in daily life, but to live from one minute to another, to eliminate from our minds everything but that which is immediately ahead of us and which demands immediate attention.

In worship, however, we are freed from the pressure of life. There are no immediate tasks to be performed: no insistent needs clamouring for immediate satisfaction. For once, we are guaranteed Time and Quietude—the rarest possessions in life today. For once, we can escape from the tyranny of the next minute with its worries, tasks and duties. And so for once, we can take a larger view of life and survey years that are past and years that are to come. We can see life as a whole, as something more than a hurried and rushed existence.

And when, as now, we do have time to take a larger view of life; when, in calm reflection, we enlarge our vision until we see life in its entirety, considerations come before us which tend to be excluded in the rush of everyday experiences. Elements in life, which at other times can receive but little of our attention, now come into the forefront of our thought. We can now allow our spiritual needs to take precedence over those material satisfactions to which, usually, we pay such high regard and to which normally we devote so large a measure of our effort. In worship, the foremost place in our consideration is given to that which develops character in man, all that which lends nobility and dignity to human life, all wherein man can express the greatness of the human spirit. We consider what it means to us and for our lives that we have been endowed by God with reason, with a power to love, with a sense of the beautiful, and with a knowledge of righteousness.

Leslie I. Edgar
Service of the Heart

The Rewards of Prayer Exceed Anticipations

The pious Jew knows from experience that the rewards of prayer exceed his anticipations. Not that God grants his every request, for God's answer is often negative. What is more, many prayers are not worthy of an answer. But the act of prayer tends to spiritualize the life of him who prays, and it tends to commit him to acts of moral significance. It helps him to discover his life's orientation and sensitizes him to the ideals and aspirations of his faith. It enables the worshiper to listen more attentively to his inner voice of conscience and paves the way for following more closely the guidelines of moral action. The devout person knows from experience that prayer is the catalytic agent that often awakens in him ethical and moral forces.

To be sure, prayer does not by itself make a man godly, but it does tend to bring man a little near to God; prayer does not automatically make one a saintly person, but it does expose him to saintly ideals. Passions and temptations overwhelm even the most constant of worshipers, but it takes greater temptations for the devout to stumble into Satan's baited trap. As Abraham Joshua Heschel has put it: "Prayer may not save us, but it makes us worthy of being saved."

Earnest prayer can help relieve anxieties of the soul and can awaken new resources of strength. It can calm the perplexities of the mind and thus endow the worshiper with new strength to overcome paralyzing fears. Prayer enables the devout to face crucial challenges and helps him to emerge from these confrontations unbroken. By sharing his frustrations and conflicts with God, the worshiper not only finds a measure of relief, but also discovers new sources of strength. When a Jew of old faced the new week on Saturday night, and his courage failed him because the anticipated trials seemed unendurable, he recited the Havdalah prayer:

> Behold, God is my salvation;
> I will trust, and will not be afraid;
> For God the Lord is my strength and song;
> And He is become my salvation (Isaiah 12:2).

From this prayer he often drew much of the strength which enabled him to face the sad uncertainties of the new week. When a paratrooper in wartime is about to jump into the vast unknown, he often feels a powerful urge to pray. And his prayer usually releases in him new sources of courage to face the dangers ahead. In time of bereavement, prayers have often enabled mourners to overcome their deep sense of loss and to rise up from the depths of their gloom to face life with revived strength and hope.

One might speculate on the psychological and even the physiological factors that accompany these phenomena. For the devout person, however, it is enough to note that on numerous occasions in his own life prayer has been eminently effective. He is therefore prepared to follow the rabbinic injunction and offer prayers even when a sword is on his neck.

Abraham Millgram
Jewish Worship

Prayer Opens Our Eyes

The Bible speaks of the becoming aware of the existence of greater power in terms of "opening of the eyes." This is the ability to see things which exist all the time but are not visible to people who are insensitive and who are unaware of the limitless layers of the creative mystery. For example, when Sarah was without child, she gave her handmaiden, Hagar, to Abraham, as a wife, according to the ancient custom, in the hope that Hagar would bear Abraham a child that Sarah, as Hagar's mistress, could claim legally to be her own. Hagar bore Ishmael to Abraham. Later, Sarah gave birth to Isaac, and she was fearful that Ishmael might gain the precedence that she wanted for the son of her own body. Sarah found reason to send Hagar and Ishmael into the desert. Hagar was desperate. She was alone in the desert with her infant son and soon found herself out of water. She prayed to God for assistance. The answer to her prayer was that "God opened her eyes." The text reads, "and she saw a well of water; and she went, and filled the bottle with water and gave the lad drink."

We are not led to believe by the biblical narrative that the well was suddenly created for Hagar. The well was there all the time, but Hagar did not see it. Through prayer, her vision and searching ability were sharpened, and she was able to see something she was unable to see before. Her eyes were "opened." She became more aware of reality. This was the answer to her prayer! Through prayer, Hagar gained the courage not to surrender and to continue her search for a solution to her problem. Prayer is a way of saying, "There must be a way out. Oh, God, show me that way!" When the verbal prayer is over, however, the person still has a role to play. He has to search for the "way out."

Herbert M. Baumgard
Judaism and Prayer

Every Genuine Prayer Lifts Man Up

According to our modern thinking there can be no question of any influence upon a Deity exalted above time and space, omniscient, unchangeable in will and action, by the prayer of mortals. Prayer can exert power only over the relation of man to God, not over God Himself. This indicates the nature and purpose of prayer. Man often feels lonely and forlorn in a world which overpowers him, to which he feels superior, and yet which he cannot master. Therefore he longs for that unseen Spirit of the universe, with whom alone he feels himself akin, and in whom alone he finds peace and bliss amid life's struggle and unrest. This longing is both expressed and satisfied in prayer. Following the natural impulse of his soul, man must pour out before his God all his desires and sighs, all the emotions of grief and delight which sway his heart, in order that he may find rest, like a child at its mother's bosom. Therefore the childlike mind believes that God can be induced to come down from His heavenly heights to offer help, and that He can be moved and influenced in human fashion. The truth is that every genuine prayer lifts man up toward God, satisfies the desire for His hallowing presence, unlocks the heavenly gate of mercy and bliss, and bestows upon man the beatific and liberating sense of being a child of God. The intellect may question the effect of prayer upon the physical, mental, or social constitution of man, or may declare prayer to be pious self-deception. The religious spirit experiences in prayer the soaring up of the soul toward union with God in consecrated moments of our mortal pilgrimage. This is no deception. The man who prays receives from the God-head, toward whom he fervently lifts himself, the power to defy fate, to conquer sin, misery, and death. "The Lord is nigh to all them that call upon Him, to all that call upon Him in truth. . . ."

Self-expression before God in prayer has thus a double effect; it strengthens faith in God's love and kindness, as well as in His all-wise and all-bountiful prescience. But it also chastens the desires and feelings of man, teaching him to banish from his heart all thoughts of self-seeking and sin, and to raise himself toward the purity and the freedom of the divine will and demand.

Kaufmann Kohler
Jewish Theology

Prayer Produces Practical Moral Results

Does prayer produce any practical moral results? I believe that it does. It is one of the consequences of our involvement with God in prayer that we come to hunger and thirst after righteousness. How else can we return the love with which we are loved? How else can we understand the meaning of the divine concern that makes us human, except by joyously translating our responding love not into merely sentimental declarations, but into specific acts of justice, decency and kindness? How else can we deal with the whole truth about ourselves, including the nasty part, except by struggling to overcome everything in ourselves and in our environment that attacks our precious God-given humanity?

In prayer, if nowhere else, we express our loyalty to the Utmost and thus achieve a clearer knowledge of our duty. When God's love becomes God's commandment, moral consequences *do* follow—not easily, not without struggle and not without the constant need for revision and rethinking, *but they follow.* And they follow not merely as *knowledge,* as the technical ability to make ethical judgments about theoretical situations and to say what is right and wrong. They follow as the courage to *be* and to *do* what our human nature with its divine dimension requires. The creative effort of prayer moves us from the *knowledge* of the good to the *deed* which is good.

Dudley Weinberg
The Efficacy of Prayer

Prayer Can Satisfy a Very Real Need of the Soul

Though our praise and our thanksgiving can confer nought upon "the Most High God, the Possessor of heaven and earth," to us it can ensure much. It can satisfy a very real need of the soul—the need to express itself to the Source of its joys, to the God of its life. Is it not true also that prayer itself begets devotion? "While we meditate the fire kindles." The payment of our tribute to God, far from removing the sense of indebtedness, leaves us more grateful, more humble than ever. In the clear atmosphere of worship we see more plainly than before the distant heights of the Divine majesty and goodness. For our own sakes, then, for the sake of the fullness it gives to our spiritual life, we must obey the natural promptings of our heart, and, like the Psalmist, "sing unto the Lord as long as we live."

Morris Joseph
Judaism as Creed and Life

We Need Prayer

God surely knows our thoughts and desires. What need is there therefore to give expression to them? This is quite true; and still the human soul yearns to give articulate expression to what is uppermost in its consciousness at any one time. Prayer does not affect God, but ourselves. In prayer, the divine within us asserts itself, seeks its union with the divine in the universe and through that becomes ennobled and glorified. God needs none of our praises and supplications, but we feel impelled to pour out our hearts to Him and by doing this we come to be in greater harmony with our spiritual selves, and with God, the spiritual element in the universe.

Julius H. Greenstone
Jewish Feasts and Fasts

If We Did Not Pray

If we did not pray, we would forget the Creator of all, and we would not know that we have a Master who rules over all, giving to all creatures their portion. But every time we pray before Him, and repent of our sins, then our prayer is heard.

Meir Aldabai
Sheveelay Emunah

The Main Intent of Prayer

But the main intent of prayer is to recognize and demonstrate that there is none in the world to whom it is fitting to pray other than God. He is the master of all the world, and we have many needs that are mentioned in our prayer. We mention them before Him in order that we may recognize that there is none who can fulfill our needs and save us from all our troubles, other than God. Upon Him we cast our burden, and we fulfill our obligation with prayer with this intent: "And God will do what is good in His eyes," whether to accept our prayers or not.

Rabbi Moshe of Trani
Bet Elohim Tefillah 2

There Is a Need to Worship

There is a need to worship in the human breast. This need finds its expression in the abasement of the savage before his totem pole, as well as in more refined types of worship. And unless this need is directed to the worship of the Supreme Being, the Source of all goodness, it will emerge in such obnoxious forms as the deification of the State and the apotheosis of the dictator, as the history of modern totalitarian movements has shown. In the year 1913, J.B. Bury published his *A History of Freedom of Thought,* in which religion is attacked in the name of freedom. It is not without significance that, in his epilogue to the 1952 edition, H. J.

Blackham feels obliged to point out that much has happened since 1913. He notes that psychologists, who have been the deadliest critics of the objective truth of religious dogmas, have also been witnesses to the necessity of religion, and that the leader figure of the political religions is a substitute for the father whom most people cannot do without and whom the traditional religions provide in a time-honored and much safer and more satisfactory way.

Louis Jacobs
Jewish Prayer

Prayer Allows Us to Be Alone with God

To feel the proximity of God we need intervals of withdrawal from other men. If we are not to lose ourselves in that real loneliness which is remoteness from God, we must have periods of loneliness upon earth when our soul is left to itself and we are remote from other men. If we are not to go astray in the world, we must look into ourselves and remember our souls and God. In the innermost recesses of the human heart there dwells a desire for such loneliness, which, incidentally, is one of the strongest roots of asceticism. It is an historical achievement of Israel that through prayer it satisfied this human need and religious necessity. The purpose of prayer is to allow us to be alone with God and apart from other men, to give us seclusion in the midst of the world. We are to seek loneliness also in the house of God even when it is crowded with men, to be alone there also with ourselves and our God. If our life is to be filled with devoutness, we must from time to time abandon the ways of the world so that we may enjoy the peace of God.

Leo Baeck
The Essence of Judaism

The Longing for Holiness

Prayer is an absolute necessity for us and for the whole world; it is also the most sacred kind of joy. The waves of our soul beat ceaselessly on the shores of consciousness. We desire of ourselves and of the whole world the kind of perfection that the limitation of existence renders impossible. In our despair and frustration we are likely to turn against our better judgment and against our Creator. But before this cancer of the spirit has had time enough to grow in our midst, we come to pray. We give utterance to our thoughts and are uplifted to a world of perfect existence. Thus our inner world is rendered perfect in truth, and restful joy fills our consciousness.

Abraham Isaac Kook
Jewish Thought

What Moves Us to Prayer

Sometimes a man awakens from his sleep and evokes the name of the Lord. He becomes aware of all around him, full of beauty and sanctity. He realizes the significance and spirituality of all creation, its necessity and purpose, and automatically identifies himself with it. He seeks to nurture the feeling of being part of it, yearns to contribute to it, to promote its ideals and delight in its achievements, to realize the divineness of creation and to appreciate the grandeur of it. "In the beginning God created the heaven and the earth." That is prayer!

Abraham Kon
Prayer

Prayer—A Conversation between Souls

The institution of prayer is founded on man's conscious need of communion with God. The deep longing of the heart for God finds in prayer an appropriate vehicle for self-expression and an adequate measure of spiritual satisfaction. But God, too, say the rabbis, delights in the prayers of the righteous. They are the crown of His glory. He wants man to seek Him, that he may find Him. Prayer is thus the soul of man holding converse with the Soul of the universe. According to the rabbis therefore, prayer, when not a mere gesture but an actual heart–experience, enables us to break through the iron wall of materiality and reach the immediate presence of God's spirit. For prayer is not an external form, like sacrifice; nor is it a mark of virtuous living, like the practice of good deeds. It is a direct approach to the throbbing heart of the universe. When with bowed head and uplifted heart we voice our deepest spiritual needs in prayer, a larger measure of the divine somehow flows into our souls. We stand face to face with the *Shekinah*. Whether we use speech for utterance or the soul wings itself aloft in purest meditation, we are, in either case, in close communion with the Spirit that is so much akin to our own, so near us in all our yearnings and strivings, so eager to receive and answer the worthy petitions of our hearts.

Israel Bettan
Post-Biblical Judaism: Its Spiritual Note

No Sadness—Only Longing and Yearning

In meditation a man may discuss his tribulations with God: he may excuse himself for his misdeeds and implore the Lord to grant him his desire to approach nearer to God. A man's offences separate him from his Maker.

It is impossible to be a good Jew without devoting each day a portion of the time to commune with the Lord in solitude, and to have a conversation from the heart with Him.

Even though a man may feel he cannot concentrate adequately upon the theme of his meditation, he should nevertheless continue to express his thoughts in words. Words are like water which falls continually upon a rock until it breaks it through. In similar fashion they will break through a man's flinty heart.

In true meditation a man cries to the Lord like a child to his father who is about to go on a journey. There is no sadness in this weeping—only longing and yearning.

Nachman of Bratzlav
Sefer Ha-Middot

Experience Is Not Debatable

The one who prays knows, with the knowledge of experience, that beyond the visible dimensions of this world there is a hidden dimension of our existence in which something of the significance of a man's being is revealed to him, revealed to a greater or lesser degree, in keeping with the strength of the communion. It is a matter of experience, and experience, as is well known, is not debatable.

S. H. Bergman
Faith and Reason

Man Is What He Prays

Science says man is an animal. Philosophy agrees, adding that he is an animal with a mind. The Bible, however, claims more: that man is an animal with a soul. Not just an animal, nor a thinking animal, but a *praying* animal. It is in his ability to commune with God that man's uniqueness and his essence lies. Man may best be described as an animal that prays, and by whose prayers animal is transformed to angel, flesh to spirit, earth to heaven. The life of man is determined by his worship. A man is what he prays.

Samuel H. Dresner
Prayer, Humility, and Compassion

We Are Incurable "Prayers"

The Prophet Jeremiah spoke of God as the "M'kor Chaim"— "The Source of Life." The prayer of Jews has ever been an expression of their yearning for a larger, more satisfying life. People pray when they are not willing to accept defeat; when they are lonely and seek companionship; when they are weak and ill and seek better health; when they are fearful and want to be reassured; when they are guilt-laden and seek forgiveness. Those who pray, express their need and demand for a broader experience of life. Conceived in these terms, prayer is the foe of pessimism. It is a manifestation of that mind and spirit which refuses to accept a restricted view of life. Prayer is a way of saying, "I believe that the world was created in such a way that men can find fulfillment for their deeper longings. I want and shall seek my own fulfillment."

The Jew prays in the mood of the biblical affirmation of the goodness of life. Our Scripture teaches that this world is good, that man can realize his legitimate aspirations in his years on this planet. Judaism teaches that if evil seems triumphant, its victory is only temporary, and justice will prevail in the end. For the Jew, forgiveness is readily available from a merciful God who is concerned with the needs of man, and aware of man's imperfections. Our prayer, as Jews, wells up from the conditioning of a lifetime that we need not settle for an ugly, unjust, diseased, lonely life. We pray in the conviction that life can be expected to yield better answers to problems than the present situation may offer. Only the man who hopes—prays. As one poet has said, "Only men incredulous of despair beat upwards to God's throne." It was Jehudah Halevi who wrote that the Jews, in spite of their experience of persecution, are "prisoners of hope"—"*asire tikvah.*" We are incurable "prayers."

Herbert M. Baumgard
Judaism and Prayer

In Prayer We Open Ourselves

In prayer we open ourselves in self-surrender to God's judgment. We often repress our real thoughts and what is truly in our hearts. Pent up in little chambers and firmly bolted against the curious gaze of the world are the actual hopes and fears of our lives. Much pain and suffering come from the hiding of our real selves in the subconscious of our souls when we refuse to share our problems with others for fear that they may think less of us. Many a psychiatrist's couch has held the twisted, nerve-wracked soul of one who could bear the burden of his secrets no longer, so that at last it burst the evenness of his mind. In prayer we find a release for what is stored within us.

What we can say to no human being we can say to Him; what we must hide from the eyes of man we can reveal to God; what has burned within us during hours of anguish can be brought forth and laid before the altar of His presence. In the quiet of our room we can be alone with Him who fills the world. There we can feel that a friend is near who will understand all we say, listen to all our words, be patient with all our complaints. He is a friend who has endless time, endless compassion and endless strength. All our fears and regrets, our crimes and jealousies, our hatred and loves, our bitternesses and joys, our secret hopes and bitter disappointments, our fervent wishes and anxieties, our dreams and disappointments, our past failures, present sins and future apprehensions pour forth in an overflowing stream of honesty and frankness from a heart opened to Him. A confession of sin and an expression of confidence, a surrendering to God of our deepest feelings, an offering up before the Lord, in fear and trembling and hope, the story of our lives.

And then, having opened our hearts to Him and having revealed the tale of our days, we stand still and wait for Him to gather up the scattered words of our devotion, to enter the gate we have opened for Him and to make His presence felt that His judgment might prevail. It is as though we cried: "Here am I. And this is the record of my days. Look into my hopes and regrets."

"Search me, O God, and know my heart; try me and know my thought and see if there be any wickedness in me, and lead me in the way everlasting."

Samuel H. Dresner
Prayer, Humility, and Compassion

What to Cherish and Remember

In prayer we learn what to cherish. Prayer trains us to distinguish between the crooked and the straight, the darkness and the light, the false and the true, the right and the wrong, the path of God and that of Satan. The mind of the man at prayer meets the imperishable ideals of faith: peace and rigtheousness, mercy and holiness, justice and humility, love for the Torah, love for God and love for our fellow man. In the midst of worldly living, when our thoughts are scattered and our wills are weak, the Hebrew prayer book keeps before our eyes what might otherwise so easily be forgotten: "*That you go not about after your own desires and your fancies after which you go astray: that you remember and do all My commandments and be holy unto your God.*" Prayers are signposts along the way, visible even in the fog, pointing in the right direction and reminding us what to remember.

Samuel H. Dresner
Prayer, Humility, and Compassion

The Rewards of Praying

The fact is, prayer is never easy. True prayer is as demanding—at least as demanding—as the carrying on of a business conversation or the writing of a letter. It purports to be a communication with a Listener. The child and the newcomer struggle with their unfamiliarity. Devout worshipers struggle with their overfamiliarity. All men of any training or any faith are put to the greatest mental effort, I imagine, to get at any real sense of talking to God.

That being the case—since so much praying is, by the limits of human nature, doomed to fall short of what it sets out to be—the question arises, is not prayer three times a day, in forms long fixed, mere empty machinery? It might be so, perhaps, except that the synagogue always remains what it was in origin: a study hall. One learns worship by worshiping or by trying to—there is absolutely no other way. The natural outpouring of the heart in moments of crisis is not, as the romantic would imagine, prayer at its best. Those who have been through such experiences know that they find themselves reduced to incoherent shamefaced stammering. Improvised prayer is honored in Judaism, and some inspired improvisations have entered the liturgy. The fixed prayers are the base for a man to stand on, in everyday devotion and in extremity.

Daily prayer at the very least is a review of one necessary instrument of the good life as Judaism knows it. It is a duty done, a link in the chain going back to Abraham's acknowledgment of One God, a link we add as God adds a new day to time. And there is no such thing as wholly absent, wholly mechanical prayer. A glint of the light in the words and the thoughts of the Jewish liturgy falls at some instant, at several instants, into the mind of the most preoccupied worshiper. At least he is there, praying to God, so that the glints can come.

Perhaps for saints and for truly holy men fully conscious prayer is really an everyday thing. They live, in that case, in clarity that plain people do not know. For the ordinary worshiper, the rewards of a lifetime of faithful praying come at unpredictable times, scattered through the years, when all at once the liturgy glows as with fire. Such an hour may come after a death, or after a birth; it may strike after a miraculous deliverance, or on the brink of evident doom; it may flood the soul at no marked time, for no marked reason. It comes, and he knows why he has prayed all his life.

Herman Wouk
This Is My God

Prayer—Both Natural and Involuntary

The universality of the disposition to pray, whether among the primitives of the jungle or among the sophisticated intellectuals of the western world, seems to indicate that the urge to pray is a response to one of man's deepest needs. In fact, the Chasidic Jews of Eastern Europe in the eighteenth century taught that prayer was both natural and involuntary. To them, prayer was a response from within man towards a "pull" from without, a response which man could not resist even if he wished to do so.

The Chasidim did not have to "think" about the legitimacy or the efficacy of prayer. They understood it to be as much an essential part of man as is his biological urge. They spoke of man's need to pray in this fashion. "When God created the world, He invested a part of Himself (a spark) in everything that He created. These sparks now yearn to re-unite themselves with their source."

In this sense, a prayer is the yearning of the divine spark within man to join itself to more of itself. We could say in less poetic language, prayer is the effort of the better part of our nature to enlarge upon itself. The Chasidic Rabbis put it this way, "Prayer *is* God," that is, the divine communing with the divine.

We, in modern times, can hardly define prayer in more compelling terms. The symbolic imagery of our eighteenth century forebearers may embarrass us. We might find it difficult to say that prayer is a kind of spiritual magnetism operating in the world, wherein the divine source and its creatures participate in a mutual "pull" towards each other. Perhaps the language of an American psychologist-philosopher might express the thought in more acceptable terms for us. Wrote William James, "He (man) becomes conscious that this higher part (of his nature) is coterminous and continuous with a *more* of the same quality, which is operative in the universe outside of him, and which he can keep in working touch with, and, in a fashion, get on board of, and save himself. . . ."

The deepest insights of psychology and religion support each other in the understanding that man can tap infinitely deeper resources within himself than he habitually uses. Prayer is a way to the appropriation of these spiritual resources.

Herbert M. Baumgard
Judaism and Prayer

Prayer Can Remind Us of What We Ought Not Forget

One of the functions of prayer is to afford us an opportunity to become reacquainted with the uniquely human part of ourselves. To remind us that our souls—the margin of superiority which distinguishes us from all our predecessors on the ladder of life—are just as much part of and responsive to the universe as are our bodies. Most of us have had the experience of being separated from someone we love for so long a time that we weren't quite sure whether we could accurately recall the look of her face or the sound of her voice. If we allow ourselves to be separated too long or too far from our own best selves, we risk forgetfulness there too. Prayer can remind us of that which we ought not forget.

This bit of instructive dialogue appears in George Bernard Shaw's *Misalliance:*

> Mr. Tarleton: The common people never pray, My Lord, they only beg.
> Lord Summerhays: Then why do you pray?
> Mr. Tarleton: To remind myself that I have a soul!

Roland B. Gittelsohn
Man's Best Hope

The Roots of Prayer

Prayer is not, as some think, the invention of religious leaders. It preceded prophets and priests, temples and houses of prayer. Prayer is essentially the product of man's yearning for the most intimate of all human communication, for the opportunity to open his heart and his mind in adoration and supplication to the divine presence. This longing to pour out one's heart before God is natural and even necessary, provided one believes that there is a God who created the universe and is concerned with man, the crown of His creation. The roots of this yearning are to be found in man's sense of insufficiency, especially in time of stress, and in his desire to liberate himself from the burden of sin and the enslavement to evil. On a higher level there is man's eternal search for the ideal, a search which leads him to the Source of all good and of ultimate perfection. Prayer is also born of man's sense of wonder, from his awareness of God's marvelous creation and the miracles that daily bear witness to God's goodness and love. One of the introductory benedictions of the daily morning service describes the marvel of the human body and its normal functions, and it concludes with the benediction "Praised art Thou, O Lord, who healest all flesh and doest wonderfully." There are also the eternal mysteries of life and death, birth and growth, the cycles of the seasons and the recurring regeneration of man's spirit and hope. When man begins to marvel at these mysteries, he naturally exclaims, as does the Jew in his daily prayers: "We give thanks unto Thee and declare Thy praise . . . for Thy miracles, which are daily with us, and for Thy wonders and Thy benefits, which are wrought at all times, evening, morn, and noon."

Prayer is also rooted in man's response of gratitude for God's blessings of life and sustenance, health and happiness, for the power to triumph over adversity and to recover from illness. Man is grateful for the sunshine and the rain in their season, for children and grandchildren, for hope in the future and anticipation of redemption. For these normal blessings man often wants to express his gratitude to God "whose loving-kindnesses never cease." Prayer is thus the bridge between earth and heaven, between man's despair and his eternal hope, between his depression of the soul and his spiritual elation.

Abraham Millgram
Jewish Worship

Prayer Is a Mitzvah

The concept of prayers which are "commanded" is not exactly an easy concept for the modern Jew to accept. First of all, however, we must clarify the concept itself as it was traditionally understood. For you may search the Bible from the beginning to the end, assuming that the Bible is the record of God's commandments to Israel, and you will not find a single commandment which says: "Thou shalt pray!" What you will find, however, is a verse, Deuteronomy 11:13, which tells Israel "to love the Lord your God, and to serve Him with all your heart and with all your soul."

The Hebrew word in this verse, which is translated as "to serve" (*ule'ovdo*), is a word which, at one time, was primarily used in connection with the sacrificial cult. The Rabbis of the Talmud, therefore, asked about this verse: "What kind of service (*avodah*) is that which takes place in the heart?" And they answered their own question by saying: "It is prayer!" In other words, when the Torah commands us to serve the Lord with all our heart, it is really commanding us to pray. Thus prayer came to be regarded as a divine commandment, an obligation, a mitzvah.

Jakob J. Petuchowski
Dynamics and Doctrine

Purify Our Hearts to Serve Thee in Truth

Prayer can best be described in the words of the prayer book, "Purify our hearts to serve Thee in truth." Every Jewish prayer is a small Yom Kippur. It challenges us to examine our hearts and thoughts. It demands that we question ourselves—whether we have been silent when we should have spoken out; whether we have been selfish when we should have been responsive to the needs of others; whether we have been thoughtless when we should have been sensitive; whether we have pursued the hollow when we should have reached for that which can hallow our life. In this kind of prayer, we do not ask God to do our will. We accept God's challenge to fulfill His will. We confess our guilt and ask Him for strength to purify ourselves.

Ernst Simon
Tradition and Contemporary Experience

The Need for Communion with God

Judaism demands of each of us: study and action, Ma'aseh and Talmud, regarding both of them as means for communion with God. We regard this demand for Study and Practice not as one to be fulfilled only by a small professional group, who may be Jews for the rest of us. Each one of us must devote part of his day to Jewish thought and the Jewish mode of communion with God.

There may be those who feel that they can live quite happily without either religious discipline or communion with God. But they are in grave error. The restlessness which characterizes us, the confusion which has come on our times, the increasing percentage of neuroses among us, and the general unhappiness of all of us in the midst of the greatest affluence the world has yet seen, has come upon us primarily because of the lack of that sense of communion with God which made our forefathers happy in spite of their poverty and their physical suffering. We resemble most closely those little children who, not having yet learned to interpret the symptoms of weariness and hunger, cry when bedtime or mealtime comes, and yet refuse either to go to bed or take their food. Living in a gilded palace, as it were, we are still miserable, for we are essentially orphans, having lost that most precious of all values in life, the sense of the Fatherhood of God.

The feeling of deprivation grows sharper and more poignant, instead of less severe, as we grow older. The time comes to each of us when the burdens of life seem far too heavy to carry, when the brightness of youth begins to fade, and we notice the lengthening shadows which presage our end.

More than ever then do we become homesick; homesick, not for our houses or for our countries, but homesick for the universal Parent of all of us, for that deep affection which is the heart of the universe itself, for the mercy of God; yet a wall of iron has been placed between us and Him, and we cannot find Him. What greater good can a man achieve, either for himself or for the world, than to contribute his effort to piercing this wall, and bring the Father and the children once more into loving communion with one another!

Louis Finkelstein
Sabbath and Festival Prayer Book

Prayer—An Invitation to God

Worship is a way of living, a way of seeing the world in the light of God. To worship is to rise to a higher level of existence, to see the world from the point of view of God. In worship we discover that the ultimate way is not to have a symbol but *to be a symbol,* to stand for the divine. The ultimate way is to sanctify thoughts, to sanctify time, to consecrate words, to hallow deeds. The study of the word of God is an example of the sanctification of thought; the Seventh Day is an example of the sanctification of time; prayer is an example of the consecration of words; observance is an example of the hallowing of deeds. . . .

To pray is to take notice of the wonder, to regain a sense of the mystery that animates all beings, the divine margin in all attainments. Prayer is our humble answer to the inconceivable surprise of living. . . .

Prayer takes the mind out of the narrowness of self-interest, and enables us to see the world in the mirror of the holy.

The focus of prayer is not the self. Prayer comes to pass in a complete turning of the heart toward God, toward His goodness and power. It is the momentary disregard of our personal concerns, the absence of self-centered thoughts, which constitute the art of prayer. Feeling becomes prayer in the moment in which we forget ourselves and become aware of God. . . .

Prayer is an invitation to God to intervene in our lives, to let His will prevail in our affairs; it is the opening of a window to Him in our will, an effort to make Him the Lord of our soul. . . .

In crisis, in moments of despair, a word of prayer is like a strap we take hold of when tottering in a rushing street car which seems to be turning over.

Abraham Joshua Heschel
Man's Quest for God

Prayer Can Keep Ideals Vividly Alive

Prayer serves admirably to articulate men's ideals, to make them conscious of the goals which they profess, and to strengthen their determination to attain them. A study of the prayers in any of the great liturgies will reveal this emphasis upon fundamental ideals of human conduct and aspiration. Thus the Jewish prayer book glorifies the Torah as the revelation of God and as the guide to the good life for Israel and mankind. It stresses the ideals of universal peace. It underscores faith in God's government of the world and in the law of righteousness as basic to the universe.

The function of prayer, as of ritual generally, is to keep ideals such as these perpetually in the forefront of our consciousness. Unlike the multiplication table or a chemical equation which needs to be learned only once, the ideals of conduct, both personal and collective, are perpetually threatened by the inundating tides of selfishness, ignorance, and short-sightedness. Thus, there arises the tragic paradox of human behavior: while men recognize that the laws of righteousness and truth are the foundations of society without which life could not go on, there is the perpetual temptation to ignore them or to bypass them in one's own personal experience—whence comes moral disaster.

The exercise of prayer can keep these ideals vividly alive, because it is enriched by a thousand emotional chords, by well-loved words hallowed by the piety of one's ancestors, by the beauty of music more eloquent than speech, by the warmth of fellowship with one's own folk. This sense of fellowship means far more than a common membership in a congregation, or even comradeship with one's contemporaries. It means a feeling of identification with all the past generations, whose spirit lives in us, and a sense of participation in the destiny of descendants as yet unborn. A prayer that has been hallowed by the piety of the past gains in poignancy and power beyond the strength of abstract logic to defend or define.

The knowledge that the ideals we voice are echoed by our brothers brings us more than a warm emotional glow. It sustains our courage in fighting for their realization and strengthens our faith in their triumph. As the tide of petty concerns and meaningless problems sweeps in upon the strand of our lives, it becomes all the more necessary to find an island of refuge, to build a lighthouse of faith, to keep aglow the great goals of human existence. The prayers in which we enunciate our hopes for country, people, and humanity bring us courage, because we know that we are not alone, on earth as well as in heaven.

Robert Gordis
A Faith For Moderns

Prayer—The Food of the Soul

What bread is to the body, prayer is to the soul. Prayer is the food of the soul. The spiritual glow of one prayer lasts until the utterance of the next, even as the strength derived from one meal lasts until the next one.

Prayer is the wireless message between man and God.

Religion brings the soul back to God, and prayer is the means which it employs to do this. Every day we send the wireless message of prayer to God, renewing thereby our constant friendship with Him. Those who make prayer a rare practice are only acquaintances but not friends of God.

Prayer serves not only as a petition to God, but as an influence upon ourselves. Our sages, centuries ago, voiced the thought echoed by the great poet, George Meredith, who declared, "He who rises from his worship a better man, his prayer is answered." Prayer has the double charm of bringing God down to man, and lifting man upward to God.

Prayer distinguishes man from the brute. The cattle get up in the morning, are fed, and sent out to the green pastures. In the evening they are brought back to the barn, given some food, ruminate and have their bed of straw made and then go to sleep. Are there not many of us today who, like the cattle, rise in the morning, swallow our food quickly, hurry downtown, the pasture for the day, back home in the evening, ruminate in some movie house, then home again to bed, just as the beast without a word of prayer, of thanks-giving for the life God daily renews within us?

The conviction of all believers in prayer is that they are speaking to one who hears and cares for them. This is one of the strongest evidences that the quest for God is real. When one prays to God, it is, as the Rabbis put it, "Like a man who talks into the ear of his friend."

At times we get discouraged and seem to think that God is angry, and does not answer our prayers. We have asked for money, for success, for strength, and yet we have not been blessed with any of these things. God may show His kindness to us, my friends, in denying us some of the things for which we prayed and longed. But just as the parent does not and should not fulfill every wish of the child, so does the All-wise God deny us for our own good some of our petitions. The poet put it, "Not what we wish, but what we need, Oh, let Thy grace supply; the good unasked, in mercy grant; the ill, though asked, deny."

It may be that we seldom say a word of prayer. We have lost the habit, or perhaps were never taught it. We are like a home with a beautiful piano in the parlor, which is never played. We who do not pray are like that piano. We do not give forth the fine, clear notes of the spirit that lies mute and dormant in our souls.

The Reverend Doctor H. Pereira Mendes had this to say on prayer:

> God gives us much.
> Should we not give Him some time?
> Let no day pass without one prayer.
> Better one prayer than no prayer
> at all.
> Prayer should be the key to the
> morning and the bolt at night.

Herbert S. Goldstein
A Letter on Prayer

Prayer Pushes Out the Walls of Normal Existence

Prayer is not an easy way of getting God to do what He ought to do, and neither is it a way of getting Him to do what we ought to do. There is no escape from the duty that lies upon us. Prayer will not offer us a refuge from the problems that trouble us. Prayer does, however, offer us the opportunity to raise ourselves and our lives to a higher peak. Prayer, if performed in that spirit, will put us in a better position, far better equipped to deal with the harassments and the dilemmas of our lives.

Prayers takes us into a large universe. It pushes out the walls of normal existence. How small is the area in which most of us live! During our vacations, we may take trips abroad and see distant lands, but most of the time the majority of us lead lives that are local and parochial. All of us live in restricted areas of our own concerns—of our families, of our own offices and needs, of our own resentments, hates, and prejudices. How important it is that now and then we go out into the great open space of the universe and let the vast breezes that come from distant places blow in upon our confined lives. How important it is to capture for a moment the large perspective that lets us see ourselves as part of a larger universe.

Morris Adler
The Voice Still Speaks

Optimism—An Essential Ingredient of the Prayer-Mood

The experience of the Jew through the centuries, teaches us that the deeply religious person does not ultimately seek victory or success. The Jew has continued to pray in spite of centuries of persecution and seeming defeat. Why has the Jew continued to find comfort in his relationship with God under these circumstances? One answer might be in the courageous prayer of an East European Jew, who exclaimed after a pogrom, "O Lord, we will be able to bear all of our suffering, if only we know that we suffer for Thy sake!" *The primary goal of the prayer relationship is not the material well-being or success of the petitioner, but the feeling of support, understanding, and purpose. The function of prayer in time of crisis is to permit the somewhat battered soul to return to life's battles certain that, in spite of defeat in past battles, he is still a loved child of creation with strong support for future struggles and with a sympathetic ally.*

Those who are embittered by the buffeting of life might well look to the Jewish people as an example of courage that will not be denied. In spite of the insane destruction of six million European Jews by the Nazis during the last great war (one-third of the Jews in the world), the Jews have continued to believe in the essential promise of life, in the power of goodness that is God. They have not accepted suffering in a stoic way, saying, "What can we do?" Rather, have they worked to find happiness in creating the Sovereign State of Israel and elsewhere, insisting that God intends for all of his children, including the Jews, to find life meaningful. Where do the Jews get this determination to stand up, again and again, after such staggering blows dealt by hate-filled hearts? Apparently, the Jews have a training which is rare and a discipline which is unusual. The recurring optimism of the Jew is rooted in his understanding of God and in his confidence that God intends for man to live a life that is reasonably fruitful. This optimism, this demand on life, is an essential ingredient of the prayer-mood.

Herbert M. Baumgard
Judaism and Prayer

The Language of Meditation

Much have I seen with the seeing of my eyes and much have I heard with the hearing of my ears. But frequently I must close my eyes to behold revelations that are focused only through the telescope of the spirit. And often I hearken to truths spoken in the hushed corridors of solitude. How much there is to hear from choirs of silence! We track the Unseen and the Unseeable to its hiding place when we learn to speak and understand the language of meditation.

Alexander Alan Steinbach
Sabbath Queen

How Lonely God Must Be

Professor Heschel describes a trip to Poland made by a friend of his during the late 1940s. His friend, an important official, was given a large compartment on a train leaving Warsaw; and when he saw a sickly, poor Jew outside, he invited the man to share his compartment.

My friend tried to engage him (the Jewish man who shared his train compartment) in conversation, but he would not talk. When evening came, my friend, an observing Jew, recited the evening prayer, while the other fellow did not say a word of prayer. The following morning my friend took out his prayer shawl and phylacteries and said his prayer; the other fellow, who looked so wretched and somber, would not say a word and did not pray.

Finally, when the day was almost over, they started a conversation. The fellow said, "I am never going to pray any more because of what happened to us in Auschwitz. . . . How could I pray? That is why I did not pray all day."

The following morning . . . my friend noticed that the fellow suddenly opened his bundle, took out his prayer shawl and phylacteries, and started to pray. He asked the man afterward, "What made you change your mind?"

The fellow said, "It suddenly dawned upon me to think how lonely God must be; look with whom He is left. I felt sorry for Him."

Abraham Joshua Heschel
Voices of Wisdom

A Sense of Living in Ultimate Relationships

Moral dedications, acts of worship, intellectual pursuits are means in the art of sanctification of time. . . . Acts of worship counteract the trivialization of existence. Both involve the person, and give him a sense of living in ultimate relationships. Both of them are ways of teaching man how to stand alone and not be alone, of teaching man that God is a refuge, not a security.

Abraham Joshua Heschel
The Insecurity of Freedom

In Prayer the Living Man Turns to the Living God

Prayer to the One God can arise only on the basis of tension and yearning with their fear and knowledge and trust. In prayer man turns toward the exalted God "who dwells on high" but whom he knows to be near. He is the God of the farthest remoteness and yet is the One who is with man—the God to whom man may cry: "Hear my prayer!" "The Lord is nigh unto all of them that call upon him, to all that call upon him in truth" (Psalm 145:18). "Seek ye the Lord while he may be found, call ye upon him while he is near" (Isaiah 55:6). This note of certainty is coupled with a note of anxiety: "Be not far from me" (Psalm 22:12). And Judaism also knows the sorrowful and almost despairing cry: "My God, my God, why hast thou forsaken me?" (Psalm 22:2). But here too, even in this cry of doubt and despair, there yet remains the sense of filiation: "*my God.*" Whatever Judaism expresses in prayer—be it the longing to elevate one's soul to God; be it the desire for deliverance from danger and affliction or for redemption from sin and guilt; be it the desire for the gifts of life and the road to the blessing—it is always this tension between the sense of God's exaltedness and the sense of his proximity from which there rises the feeling of him who prays to God. There is thus always in it a wonderful intermingling of mystery and certainty: it is as if heaven and earth touched each other and the far God thereby became the near God. In prayer the life-impulse of the man who knows that God has created him turns toward the foundation of its existence. To the living God there turns the living man whose innermost being craves for the elevation and fulfillment of transcending the limitations of mortality. To speak of the expansion of life is thus a true word of prayer. "Out of straitness I called upon the Lord: the Lord answered me, and led me into enlargement" (Psalm 118:5).

Leo Baeck
The Essence of Judaism

Prayer Can Turn Suffering into Insight

Our needs and worries, our concerns and petitions, serve to initiate prayer and to bring us into contact with God. They begin a process which leads beyond the narrow interests of the ego and into the realms of the infinite. The real issue of prayer is not the self; indeed, it is precisely in that moment when we *forget* the self, our worries and needs, and become aware of His presence, when in the act of asking for ourselves we suddenly realize that we stand before Him who fashioned us in love, watches over us in compassion and ever seeks to enter our lives, that all our private concerns seem petty and trite. It is in that very moment that our petition turns into prayer.

A man suffering with cancer may be led to prayer. It is doubtful whether there is any relation between the words he utters for recovery and the physical condition of the cells of his body. But in devout prayer for physical recovery, he may for the first time open his heart to God, feel His presence close, gain a new strength and a new understanding of life's meaning and purpose which he never knew before. He may better withstand his illness and, perhaps, learn a lesson from it.

Prayer cannot cure cancer, but it can help us endure the suffering and it can help us turn that suffering into insight.

Samuel H. Dresner
Prayer, Humility, and Compassion

Words We Speak to God Can Affect Words We Speak to Man

Moreover, said Levi Yitzhak, the words a man utters to God have the power to lift up to Heaven the words he later speaks to his fellowman. The nobility of spirit to which a man ascends during the hour of his worship exalts him even afterward when he goes out among his neighbors to attend to his daily affairs. Thus, upon concluding the *Amidah* prayer, when we take leave of the King of kings, moving three steps backward and bowing, we say, "O God, guard my tongue from evil and my lips from speaking guile. . . ." For prayer to God with words that are pure and true and come from the depths of the soul will keep a man from frivolous speech afterward, since he will then say to himself, "Only a moment ago I uttered words before the great and awesome King. In a few hours I will again pray to Him Whose glory fills the world. How, then, dare this very same mouth speak wasteful, meaningless words now?"

Samuel H. Dresner
Levi Yitzhak of Berditchev

The Dignity and Meaning of Our Divine Service

Life robs us of the correct judgment concerning God, the world, man, and Israel, and concerning our own relationship to them all. Leaving the disturbing influences of life, and turning to God, you can find it again through the contemplation that is part of *Tefillah.* All the various component parts of worship serve this great purpose. There are *Tehilloth,* the psalms or praises; they show us God as He is revealed in nature, in the world of man and in Israel, and *Tefilloth,* the prayers or devotions, which help us evaluate our own personalities and our role in this world on the basis of these concepts. There are *Todoth,* prayers of thanksgiving, and *Bekashoth,* supplications, which express our full and unreserved acknowledgment that everything past or future proceeds from His hands, and the acknowledgment of the errors and failings of our own lives. The *Techinoth* express our struggle to rise up once more from the depths of our weaknesses and backslidings. The foundation and basis upon which all this edifice of worship is raised is the *Keriath Hatorah,* the Reading of the Law, which imparts to us the instruction and wisdom which we require. Its utmost summit and goal, the perfect fruit of our piety, are the *Berachoth,* benedictions, the firm resolutions to promote the fulfillment of God's will in the midst of everyday, active life. Retain these sketchy outlines in your mind, and bearing them in memory, contemplate afresh our prayers, our Divine service as a whole, and see if you do not find it more dignified, meaningful and important than you had ever before imagined.

Samson Raphael Hirsch
Nineteen Letters

3 WHEN AND HOW TO PRAY

Whenever there rises in man's heart a joyous thought, a feeling of happiness, a sense of love for His law, that moment is auspicious for prayer.

Zevi Hirsch Kaidanover
Kav Ha-Yashar

What Is an Acceptable Time?

R. Jose b. Chalafta taught: There are proper times for prayer, as it says, "As for me, let my prayer come before Thee at an acceptable time" (Psalm 49:13). What is an "acceptable time"? When the community is at prayer. Therefore a man should rise early to pray, for nothing is greater than the power of prayer.

Tanchuma Bereishit, Miketz

Waiting for the Spirit to Move Us

A musician must practice by prearranged schedule, regardless of his inclination at the moment. So with the devout soul. It may not rely on caprice or put its hope in chance. It must work. The man on the other hand who folds his hands, waiting for the spirit to move him to think of God—who postpones worship for the right mood and the perfect setting, a forest or mountain peak, for example—will do little of meditating or praying. After all, how often does one find himself in a "cathedral of nature," and when he does who shall say that he will be in a worshipful temper?

Milton Steinberg
Basic Judaism

Keeping Alive Our Ability to Pray

A writer, whether he feels like it or not, may on occasion force himself to abide by the ancient rule, *nulla dies sine linea*, not to let a single day pass without writing at least one line, for he knows that the lack of practice will make it so much harder for him to write even if, on some future occasion, he may again "feel like" writing. Much the same can be said about the athlete who has to keep in shape, and about the musician who has to maintain his mastery of his chosen instrument. And just as the writer, and the athlete, and the musician may not always be "in the mood" to practice their skills, so the Jew may not always be "in the mood" to pray. Yet, if the Jew were to make his praying entirely dependent upon his moods, he may find soon enough that he has lost the ability to pray, to be on intimate terms with the Sovereign of the Universe—even if, one day, circumstances should produce the "mood" in which prayer is felt to be desirable. Prayer as an "obligation" keeps alive our ability to pray.

In his book, *Man's Quest for God*, Professor Abraham Joshua Heschel describes his spiritual anguish while studying at the University of Berlin after having spent his childhood in the pietistic environment of Eastern Europe. A new and different world was opened up to him here. One evening, as he was walking through the streets of Berlin, it suddenly struck him that the sun had gone down, that evening had arrived. But sunset, in the Jewish tradition, is associated with the recitation of the evening *Shema*; and young Heschel began to utter the words of the benedictions preceding the evening *Shema*. Uttering those words, he began to find himself again as a Jew, as a human being in God's world. It was the "duty to worship" which reminded his distraught mind that it was time to think of God. He would not have done so otherwise. And Heschel confesses:

> I am not always in a mood to pray. I do not always have the vision and the strength to say a word in the presence of God. But when I am weak, it is the law that gives me strength; when my vision is dim, it is duty that gives me insight.

Jakob J. Petuchowski
Dynamics and Doctrines

When Prayer Is Divine Service of the Heart

When a man, overwhelmed by the impact of a specific experience, seeks the nearness of God or bursts forth in halleluyah or bows down in gratitude, it is prayer but not service of God yet; it is a human response to a potent stimulus. But when he prays without the stimulus of a specific occasion, acknowledging that man is always dependent on God, that independently of all personal experience God is always to be praised and to be thanked, then—and only then—is prayer divine service of the heart. It is noteworthy that, whereas Judaism is life under the law of God, the Halakha casts a somewhat ambiguous light on obligatory prayer. Most of the authorities maintain that the obligation to pray is not a biblical law but was instituted by the rabbis. Maimonides seems to stand alone in his opinion that prayer is prescribed by the Bible. However, even according to him, the times of prayer, the number of prayers or their nature and contents, were left to be determined by man. It would seem to us that the ambiguity of the place that prayer has acquired in the system of Halakha reflects its essential quality. Prayer in its original free and personal form cannot be obligatory. No law can be imposed on the outpouring of the heart. The heart prays when and the way it must because of its own inner necessity. But such praying has its problematic aspects. In order to remove them, it calls for obligatory prayer. Obligatory prayer emerges out of the inadequacies of spontaneous prayer. It is an obligation which arises out of a human activity that represents a vital manifestation of religious living but which yet cannot be prescribed. Prayer, which is always of the heart or else it is not prayer, calls for the service of the heart.

Eliezer Berkovits
Studies in Torah Judaism

A man should know that during his prayers he stands in the King's palace and sees only the King. He will then forget his own existence.

Nachman of Bratzlav
Likutay Etzot Ha-Shem

A Single Word

Make it a habit to seclude yourself in prayer, expressing your thoughts before God each day. If all you can say is a single word, it is still very good. If you can only say one word, repeat it over and over again. Even if you spend many days repeating this word, it is also good. Repeat the word innumerable times. God will eventually have mercy and open your lips so that you will be able to express yourself.

Nachman of Bratzlav
Likutay Etzot Ha-Shem

Inspired by Love

Worship inspired by fear is worship, but it does not rise to the highest part of the supernal sphere. That is reserved for worship inspired by love.

The Zohar

A Vain Prayer

One who cries out regarding something that is passed, this is a vain prayer. For example, if one's wife is pregnant and he says, "May it be His will that she give birth to a son," this is a vain prayer. If one is coming from a journey and hears a cry in the city, and says, "May it be His will that this not be my household," this is a vain prayer.

Berachot 9:3

The Prayer of the Sick Person Is Better

It is written (Genesis 21:17), "And God heard the voice of the young boy."

From here we see that the prayer of the sick person himself is better than that which others pray for him, and it is accepted first.

Rashi on Genesis 21:17

The First Step to Prayer

For prayer to have real significance, man when praying must disengage himself from mundane, everyday affairs, and must detach himself from the shallow and humdrum materialism which engulfs him when he is engaged in his ordinary daily activities. By doing so, he will reach that vital degree of awareness of the divine side of his existence which is the turning point in his innermost being. That turning point marks the striving of the suppliant, for it lies in the very depths of his heart. When man attains that degree of awareness and is capable of withdrawing from his habitual pedestrianism, he has taken the first step to prayer.

Abraham Kon
Prayer

God wants the heart.
Sanhedrin 106b

Spontaneous Prayer Is Permissible

It is perhaps imperative today, now that the Hebrew language has been revived and the Jewish people has reestablished its State, to publicize the fact that spontaneous prayer is permissible and has its place at the conclusion of the regular Tefillah. Completely standardized prayer is always in danger of becoming a mechanical and perfunctory performance. Hence the individual should be given the opportunity to break the barriers restraining the spontaneous effusion of his feelings before his Creator. Perhaps the need could be fulfilled by the choice of appropriate Psalms in which the loneliness of the individual finds expression.

B. S. Jacobson
Meditations on the Siddur

A Joyous Heart

The root of all prayer is a joyous heart before God, as it is written (1 Chronicles 16:10), "Glory in His holy name, let the heart of those who seek God rejoice."

It is for this reason that King David played the harp with all his prayers and psalms, in order to fill his heart with joy, in his love of God.

Yehuda He-Chasid
Sefer Chasidim 18

A Time to Shorten Prayers

When the children of Israel came to the Red Sea, and Moses prayed long, the Holy One said to him: "My children are in trouble, the sea before them and the enemy behind them, and you stand here indulging in prayer!"

Eliezer ben Hyrcanus
MeKilta, Beshalach

Whom God Will Not Reject

Rabbi Joshua Ben Levi said: When the temple stood, a person could bring a sacrifice, and he had the merit of that particular sacrifice. But one who is humble in spirit, is counted as if he brought all the sacrifices. It is thus written (Psalm 51:19a), "The sacrifices to God are a broken spirit." And not only that, but his prayer is not rejected. It is thus written (Psalm 51:19b), "A broken and oppressed heart, God will not reject."

Sanhedrin 43b

Three Fitting Things

The chasidic rabbi, Menachem Mendel of Premislan, once declared: "Three things are fitting for us: upright kneeling, motionless dancing, and silent screaming."

Kneeling is not only a matter of physical posture: it can also be a spiritual attitude. Thus we can kneel even when we are upright. A man can stand erect and feel humility and reverence in his heart.

Dancing is not only a matter of outward movement; it can also be an inner mood. We can dance motionless.

Prayer is not always articulate; often it is the unspoken yearning alone. We can cry out silently.

Sidney Greenberg
Likrat Shabbat

Include in your prayer for your own sick all the sick.
Chanina ben Hama
Shabbat 12b

The Power of Tears

There was a case where Rabbi Eliezer decreed 13 fasts for the community and rain did not fall. In the end, the people began to leave. He said, "Have you prepared graves for yourselves?" All the people began to wallow in tears. Rain then fell.

Taanit 25b

Preparation for Prayer

When the rabbis established the "Order of the Prayers," they foresaw the danger of the prayers becoming mere mouthings of fixed formulas. To meet this danger they not only provided for personal prayers, but they also insisted on due preparation. "The pious men of old," says the Mishnah, "used to wait an hour before praying in order that they might concentrate their thoughts upon their Father in Heaven" (Berachot 5:1). The rabbis realized that a man cannot possibly make the transition from business transactions or idle talk to reverent prayer quickly. Nor can one spontaneously cross over from grief to exultation. The Talmud therefore teaches that a person whose mind is not at ease must not pray. One of the sages, relates the Talmud, would not pray when he was agitated (Eruvin 65a). A bridge of preparation is indispensable.

In later centuries special prayers were composed to aid in "directing the heart to God," such as the introductory supplications known as Reshuyot, which ask permission to recite the prayers that follow. The medieval Hebrew poets Solomon Ibn Gabirol and Judah Halevi excelled in their elaborate introductions. The recitation of the Ashre (Psalm 145) during the afternoon service was meant to induce the worshipers to meditate awhile before beginning the essential service itself. It is related that the Tzanzer Rebbe was asked by one of the Hasidim: "What does the Rebbe do before praying?" "I pray," said he, "that I may be able to pray properly."

Abraham Millgram
Jewish Worship

All of Us Need These Moments

Before one can pray, he must realize, as did our father, Jacob, that "The Gate of Heaven" is here, wherever one is. We must pray where we are, with what we have. You cannot pray while frantically running. The person who wishes to pray must find a quiet place to rest. When Rebekah first met Isaac, he was in the field, meditating, praying. The biblical text reads, "And Isaac went out to meditate in the field at the eventide . . ." (Genesis 24:63). No doubt, he went to get away from the burdens of his daily business, to separate himself, if but momentarily, from the small talk of friends and servants, to be alone with himself and with God (Berachot 26b). All of us, especially in our modern, harried world, need these moments when we can walk away from our burdens and commune with the vastness of the universe. In such a situation, we can come to understand that all of the things we think to be of prime importance are really but ripples on the ocean of life. In moments like these, the soul is refreshed, and our perspective of life is enlarged. Comparable to the nature of this prayer-moment is the calm we feel when we gaze at the sea for a period of time. The huge expanse of the water, the regularity of its movements, the limitlessness of the vision, soon bring us "out of ourselves," and the calm of the sea, its power and stability, become part of us, and we become part of it. Gazing at a natural object like the sea, we can gain an insight into the calm and power of its Creator. As we think of the limitless power of our Creator, we are moved to "adoration," and in praising Him, we empty ourselves of our miseries and take part of His calm and power into ourselves.

Herbert M. Baumgard
Judaism and Prayer

I believe with perfect faith that it is only proper to pray to God, and that it is not proper to pray to anything else.

Moses Maimonides
The Thirteen Articles of Faith

Ten Expressions for Prayer

There are ten expressions for prayer: Cry out, cry, groan, distress, lamentation, intercession, falling down, praying, entreaty, standing up, placate, beseech: *Cry out* in Egypt, for we read: And it came to pass in the course of those many days that the king of Egypt died; and the children of Israel sighed by reason of the bondage, and cried out for help (Exodus 2:23); *cry*—as it says: And their cry under bondage came up to God (Exodus 2:23); *groaning*—And God heard their groaning (Exodus 2:24); *distress*—In my distress I called upon the Lord (Psalm 18:7); *lamentation*—Neither lift up lamentation for them (Jeremiah 7:16); *intercession*—Neither make intercession to Me (Jeremiah 7:16); *falling down*—And I fell down before the Lord as at the first (Deuteronomy 9:18); *praying*—And I prayed unto the Lord (Deuteronomy 9:26); *entreaty*—And Isaac entreated the Lord for his wife (Genesis 25:21); *standing up*—Then stood up Phinehas and interposed (Psalm 106:30); *placating*—But Moses set himself to placate the Lord (Exodus 32:11); *beseech*—And I besought the Lord.

Sifre Deuteronomy, Va'etchanen

As the palm and the cedar strain upwards, so the heart of the righteous is directed towards God.

Genesis Rabbah 41:1

The Main Thing

The main thing in worship is the feeling of oneness with God, the ecstasy with which one serves Him and studies Torah, the attitude which is free of selfish motivation.

The Baal Shem Tov

God's Delight

Our prayers are not exercises in reading aloud. They express Jewish devotion, Jewish hope, a reaching out for God. So too our singing. Sour notes, poor voices—these God forgives. The whole-hearted response of His people—this is His delight.

Joseph H. Hertz
Daily Prayer Book

Jewish prayer means praying in Hebrew.
Franz Rosenzweig
Letter to Gershom Scholem

Pay Attention, Take Care

The worshiper must direct his heart to each word that he says. He is like a man who walks in a garden collecting rare and precious flowers, plucking them one by one in order to weave a garland. So we move from word to word and from page to page uniting the words into prayers. Every word seizes hold of us and cleaves to us and entreats us not to abandon it and says: "Consider my light, notice my grace. Pay attention as you take hold of me, take care as you pronounce my name."

Nachman of Bratzlav
Likutay Etzot Ha-Shem

One sigh uttered in prayer is of more avail than all the choirs and singers.

Samuel J. Agnon
Israel Argosy No. 3

We Can Pray in Silence

The Tzartkover Rebbe failed to preach for a long time. He was asked why, and he replied: "There are seventy ways of reciting the Torah. One of them is through silence."

Perhaps the Rebbe was trying to convey the thought that we teach best not by our exhortations but by our examples, not by our lessons but by our lives.

If we can teach silently we can also pray silently. The Psalmist tells us: "To You, silence is praise."

We can praise in silence; we can petition in silence; we can pray in silence.

Sidney Greenberg
Likrat Shabbat

Rav Judah made it a practice to dress himself up before he prayed because it is said: "Worship the Lord in the beauty of holiness" (Psalm 29:2).

Berachot 30b

Do Not Laugh

Do not laugh at one who moves his body,
 even violently, during prayer.
If a man is drowning in a river,
 he makes all kinds of motions
 to try to save himself.
This is not a time for others to laugh.

Likkutim Yekarim 15a
Arthur Green
Barry Holtz
Your Word Is Fire

Rabbi Elazar made it a practice to recite a new prayer every day. Rabbi Abuhu recited a new blessing every day.

Yerushalmi, Berachot 4:3

Prayer—A Creative Enterprise

The Talmud reflects its concern with meaningful worship in a discussion as to what is perfunctory prayer. A variety of answers is given: "Rabbi Jacob bar Iddi said: 'Whoever finds his praying a burden.' The Sages say: 'Whoever does not offer it in a spirit of entreaty.' Rab Joseph said: 'Whoever cannot add any element of novelty to it.' Abba bar Abin and Hanina bar Abin said: 'Whoever does not pray as the sun is setting' (Berachot 29b)." In these utterances of the Sages, the truth is emphasized that true prayer should bring us a sense of relief from burden, an easing of the spirit, an exaltation of the mind. It must be the result of a constant striving for close contact with the Source of our being. It must be a creative enterprise, marked by a perpetual search after new forms of expression. It must be accessible to us, as the shadows fall.

When we succeed in mastering the act of prayer, we can face the twilight of life, its tragedy and trials, and yet look hopefully for the dawn. As we ascend the ladder of prayer, we shall feel the ecstasy of the youthful Jacob at Beth-El: "Indeed, the Lord is in this place, though I did not know it."

Robert Gordis
The Ladder of Prayer

The Root of Prayer—Intimate Reliance on Him

With its incomparable ability to hear the finest nuances of the Hebrew text, the Midrash interprets the words of the psalmist, "Give ear to my words, O Eternal One, consider my meditations," as referring to two different forms of prayer: the one uttered in words, the other silently embedded in the heart. Elaborating the phrase of the psalm, it is explained: "David prayed to God: Creator of the universe! When I have the strength to stand before Thee in prayer and to utter my words, do listen; but when I am without strength, consider Thou what is in my heart, consider my meditation." One should pray in a synagogue. But Rabbi Eliezer ben Yaakob, one of the great Tannaim, taught: ". . . if you cannot go to the synagogue, pray in your field; if you cannot pray in the field, pray in your house; if you cannot pray in your house, pray on your bed; and if you are unable to do that either, meditate in your heart, as it is written: 'Speak in your heart upon your bed, and be still.'" To dwell in silence before God may also be praying, for the root of prayer is neither informing God, nor asking Him; but, in intimate reliance on Him, making him the confidant of our heart.

Eliezer Berkovits
Studies in Torah Judaism

Getting Ready to Pray

Our sages affirmed that before one recites his prayers, he should put himself in a proper state physically. They learn this from the words of Amos, "Prepare to meet thy God, O Israel" (Amos 4:12).

Berachot 23a

How to Come before the King

The Psalmist says:
"A prayer of a poor man"—
But the text may also read:
"A prayer *to* a poor man!"

Though the treasure houses of the king are full,
they are managed by the king's officials.
Having nothing to do with all his treasures,
the king himself is like a poor man.

He who comes in search of treasure
will never see the King.
Only one who seeks no riches,
who prays as to a poor man,
can come before the King Himself.

Toledot Ya'akov Yosef 169b
Arthur Green
Barry Holtz
Your Word Is Fire

The Prayer That Ascends on High

Prayer, if offered from the heart and for the sake of heaven, even though the worshipper does not know its meaning, ascends on high and pierces the firmament.

The Baal Shem Tov

Learn From a Laborer

He who is about to pray should learn from a common laborer, who sometimes takes a whole day to prepare for a job. A woodcutter, who spends most of the day sharpening the saw and only the last hour cutting the wood, has earned his day's wage.

Mendel of Kotzk
quoted by Martin Buber in
Tales of the Hasidim

If you are not at peace with the world, your prayer will not be heard.

Nachman of Bratzlav
Sefer Ha-Middot

The Search for Silence midst Noise

Prayer is the search for silence midst noise. Life is so filled with tumult that we do not hear ourselves. Failing to hear the voice of our spirit, can we hear the voice of God?

There are voices that can be heard only in silence. The artist and thinker withdraw to privacy to create and meditate. The poet seeks solitude to hear the melodies of his soul. The solitary stroller in the woods hears music that would go unheard midst noise. The silences of the night would lose their eloquence in the glare. There are symphonies that are audible only to the undistracted and the silent.

Morris Adler
Shaarey Zedek Recorder

When is prayer heard? When the soul is subdued.

Al-Harizi
Tachkemoni

The Heart Must Know

Let those who do not know Hebrew learn the prayers in their own vernacular, for prayer must be understood. If the heart does not know what the lips utter, it is no prayer.

Sefer Chasidim

R. Ammi said: Man's prayer is not accepted unless he puts his heart in his hands.

Taanit 8a

With Joy and Trembling

When one stands up to say the Tefillah, he should do so in a reverent frame of mind. What is the Scriptural source for this? Rabbi Nahman ben Isaac said: We learn it from here: "Serve the Lord with fear and rejoice with trembling" (Psalm 2:11). What is meant by "rejoice with trembling?" Rabbi Adda ben Mattena replied in the name of Rab: In the place where there is rejoicing, there should also be trembling.

Berachot 30b

Our Sages Did Not Make Prayer Fixed and Unchangeable

Our forebears, of blessed memory, established for us the norm for prayers—how to praise God and how to pray before Him. They did not, however, intend with their regulation to make the form of prayer fixed and unchangeable, to make it impossible to add or subtract. . . . Our Sages did not put in writing our prayers and blessings in book form. Contrariwise, they said: "They who write down Benedictions (prayers) commit as gross a sin as those who burn the Torah." They permitted each individual and each cantor to lengthen or shorten (the prayer) in accordance with his wisdom. Therefore they decreed that the Eighteen Benedictions are to be recited silently so that the reader can organize his prayer in the meantime before he recites it aloud before the people (see Rosh Hashanah 34b). That is why R. Eliezer said (Berachot 4:4), "He who recites his prayer in a routine manner, his prayer cannot be a supplication for God's grace."

Samuel David Luzzatto
Machzor B'nai Roma

Pray Only in a Room Which Has Windows

R. Chiya b. Abba said in the name of R. Yochanan: A man should only pray in a room which has windows, since it says (Daniel 6:11): "Now his windows were open in his upper chambers towards Jerusalem" (Berachot 34b). Prayer is indeed a service, personal and individual to the worshipper. Yet a precondition to its completeness is his recognition of the outside world around him. Anyone, whose individualized worship of the heart leads him to withdraw from any connection with the outside world, will not attain perfection in prayer, and this is necessary for man's revival, to infuse in him the Divine spirit which will lead him to act and to be influenced by justice and righteousness.

Hence man should not pray in a house where there are no windows.

The ability to look outside will arouse him to an awareness of his duty and his relationship to the totality of the world in which he lives. His relationship to the outside world should consist in working towards true happiness, the knowledge of the true fear of God, and general peace; and this is the function of Jerusalem from which God's word emanated.

Abraham Isaac Kook
Olat Re'iyah

Prayer is meaningless unless it is subversive, unless it seeks to overthrow and to ruin the pyramids of callousness, hatred, opportunism, falsehoods.

Abraham Joshua Heschel
God in Search of Man

Silence before God Is as Appropriate as Prayer

To believe in God is usually associated in our minds with praying to Him. Actually, silence before Him is at least as appropriate a stance. There are two possible reasons for such a silence, one which results from the nature of man, the other which results from the nature of God.

In the first sense, man's most profound emotions, his deepest needs and highest aspirations are embedded so tightly in the mine of his soul that the pick-axe of words cannot quite reach them. If God is to take cognizance of them at all, man can do no more than simply stand before Him and confidently hope that, out of His power and goodness, He will concern Himself with them. Psalm 4:5: "Commune in your hearts on your beds and be still!" Psalm 139:4: "There is no word on my tongue, but You, O God, know it all." It is in this kind of silence that lovers sit and perhaps hold hands, exchanging no vocal expressions but drinking in one another's presence. It is also this kind of silence that prevails between members of a family who have just lost a common and beloved relative: they look at one another and, weeping, perhaps bemoan their loss, but words could neither help them nor properly express their sentiments.

Such silence is itself due to two causes. In the first place, what goes on in the heart is so powerful, so inchoate, and so deeply chiseled into the flesh that even if it could be lifted out of its setting, it would break the delicate vessels of any words into which it might be put. In the second place, speech requires distance between the speaker and him who is addressed. None would think of using the telephone to communicate with a person who is sitting in the same room. Even so, we do not talk with anyone who is in our hearts. He knows what we feel while we feel it.

Steven Schwarzschild
Judaism

Prayer should not be recited as if a man were reading a document. R. Aha said: A new prayer should be said every day.

Yerushalmi, Berachot 4:3

Prayer amid Grass and Trees

Meditation and prayer before God is particularly efficacious in grassy fields and amid the trees, since a man's soul is thereby strengthened, as if every blade of grass and every plant united with Him in prayer.

Nachman ben Simcha

When wood burns it is the smoke alone that rises upwards, leaving the grosser elements below. So it is with prayer. The sincere intention alone ascends to heaven.

The Baal Shem Tov

Even the Humblest Can Commune with God

Through the power of prayer, even the humblest of men can converse and commune with God. Every outpouring of the heart, when uttered with fervor and devotion, is a true prayer. Every hour is the hour of prayer, and every hut and forest is a house of God. All that is necessary is that we pray with a realization of its spiritual inwardness. All that is necessary is that we pray with passion and sincerity. All that is necessary is that we pray with joy in our hearts.

The Baal Shem Tov

The Language of Prayer

The significance of the prayers consists not alone in their content but also in their traditional forms, in the verbiage in which they have been bequeathed to us, hence, also in the Hebrew language. This must remain, therefore, with few exceptions, the language of prayer.

Abraham Geiger
Israelitisches Gebetbuch

God Must Be Served with Joy

Rabbi Levi Yitzhak was a master of prayer. Prayer was a discipline by which he ordered his hours, a mystery to which he surrendered his soul, and a meaning with which he struggled all his life to comprehend. Some of the noblest passages in his writings deal with prayer.

He taught, for example, that melancholy contracts the spirit, weakens the soul, and dims the divine light that burns within; it is the fruit of selfishness and denotes an absence of gratitude to God for the marvels of the simplest facts of life and for the wonder of life itself. Melancholy is tantamount to denial of the goodness of God and stands as a wall between Heaven and earth, defeating the purposes of prayer. The opposite of melancholy is joy. God must be served with joy, Rabbi Levi Yitzhak said, and this was a characteristic of his own service. Indeed, his grandson, the Rabbi of Neshkhiz, remarked that it was in part due to the quality of joy in which Levi Yitzhak immersed himself that the great power of his prayers was manifest.

In truth the Holy One, blessed be He, desires to pour out His love upon the Children of Israel at every moment and at every hour, but the Evil One prevents this. When Israel is aroused in joy, however, then the power of this joy dispels the power of the Evil One, and a mighty flood of divine love flows forth unimpeded.

Samuel H. Dresner
Levi Yitzchak of Berditchev

Make the Heart Soft

"O Thou that hearest prayer, unto Thee shall all flesh come" (Psalm 65:3). Why does it say, "all flesh," and not all men? The wise have used this verse to teach that man's prayer is heard only if he make his heart soft as flesh.

Midrash Tehillim 65:3

Without Ulterior Motive

When the Torah says, "Serve Him with all your heart," the main intent is to command that all our service of God be with all our hearts. The complete intent should be for His name, without any ulterior motive. One should not observe the commandments without feeling, or in order to obtain some personal benefit.

Nachmanides
Commentary on Sefer Ha-Mitzvot

What Is Devotion?

What then is devotion? One must free his heart from all other thoughts and regard himself as standing in the presence of God. Therefore, before engaging in prayer, a man ought to go aside for a little in order to bring himself into a devotional attitude, and then he should pray quietly and with feeling, not like one who carries a weight and goes away. Then after prayer the worshipper ought to sit quiet for a little and then depart.

Moses Maimonides
Guide for the Perplexed

Before We Begin to Pray

Before one begins his prayers, and especially in the morning service, he should accept upon himself the mitzvah to love his neighbor as himself. He should keep in mind that he loves everyone of Israel as his own self. In this way his prayer will include all Israel. It will have the capacity to ascend, to bear fruit, and to achieve success.

Isaac Luria
quoted by Joseph H. Hertz in
Daily Prayer Book

God Only Requires Words or Tears

The people of Israel say, "We are poor. We have no sacrifices to bring as an offering."

God replies, "I need only words, as it is written, 'Take with you words' (Hosea 14:2). This refers to words of Torah."

The people say, "But we do not know words of Torah."

God replies, "Weep and pray, and I will receive you."

Shemot Rabbah 38:4

You Must Concentrate

Arouse your concentration and remove all disturbing thoughts from your mind, so that when you pray, your thoughts will be pure.

If you were speaking to an earthly king, who is here today and tomorrow in the grave, you would be careful with your words, concentrating on each one, lest you say something wrong. When you pray, you are speaking before the King of kings, the Blessed Holy One. You must concentrate all the more. God probes all thoughts, and before Him, thought is the same as speech.

Pious men of old used to meditate and concentrate in prayer until they divested themselves of the physical. They attained a spiritual strength almost on the level of prophecy.

Yaakov ben Asher
Tur Orach Chayim

Strength Enters the Words

You must force yourself to pray. Some people say that prayer must be totally spontaneous, without being forced, but they are wrong. You must force yourself to direct all your power into your prayer.

Nevertheless, when you pray with true devotion, binding thought to word and listening carefully to your own words of prayer, then strength will automatically enter your worship. All your faculties will anticipate their being drawn into words of holiness. When you focus your mind on your prayers, this strength enters the words.

Merely concentrate on the words, and strength will enter your prayers without your having to force it.

Nachman of Bratzlav
Sefer Ha-Middot

The Length of Prayers

A disciple descended before the pulpit in the presence of Rabbi Eliezer and prayed at great length. The other disciples said, "Master, see how profuse he is!" He replied, "Is he any more profuse than Moses, who prayed for 'forty days and forty nights' (Deuteronomy 9:25)?"

In another instance, a disciple descended before the pulpit in the presence of Rabbi Eliezer and prayed very briefly. The other disciples said, "Master, how brief he is!" He replied, "Is he any briefer than Moses, who prayed, 'O God heal her' (Numbers 12:13)?"

Berachot 34a

The Essence of Prayer

Even though we follow the order of worship ordained by the Great Assembly, personal prayer, as it originally existed, is still the most beneficial. Make a habit of praying before God from the depths of your heart, using your own words, in whatever language you know best. Ask God to make you truly worthy of serving Him. This is the essence of prayer.

Nachman of Bratzlav
Likutay Etzot Ha-Shem

Pray with a Melody

When you pray, do so with a melody that is pleasant and sweet in your ears. The melody will cause you to pray with feeling, since it leads your heart to follow the words.

When you ask God for something, use a melody that fortifies the heart, and when you utter God's praise, use one that makes the heart rejoice. Your lips will then be filled with love and joy before God, who gazes into your heart. You will be able to bless Him with abundant love and joy.

Yehuda He-Chasid
Sefer Chasidim

We Must Understand Our Prayers

It is not fitting that we pray and weave the crown of the Life of worlds in any language other than Hebrew, the Holy Tongue with which the universe was created.

The only exception is the person poor in knowledge, who does not know Hebrew, he should express his thoughts before God Himself. God sees into the heart, and has more pleasure from contrite prayer in other languages than from prayer without feeling, even though it may be said in Hebrew. It is obvious that it is impossible to have feeling unless one understands what he is saying.

Menachem Azariah Da Fano
Kanfay Yonah

One must shake during prayer, since it is written, "All my bones shall say, O God, who is like You"(Psalm 35:10). This is the custom of the righteous.

Midrash
Menorat Ha-Maor

In What Language Shall We Pray?

The function of worship is not only to commune with God. If that were its sole purpose, there would be no need for *public* worship. In worshiping as a congregation, we seek a sense of fellowship with those who share our religious tradition. The sense of togetherness which is effected by public worship is of incalculable worth in laying the basis for communion with the Divine. The interdependence of the elements of a civilization—peoplehood, culture, and religion—is as evident in respect to worship as in respect to all other aspects of Jewish life. In worship, the whole of us should be engaged. When we pray as Jews, therefore, our worship must express our self-identification with the Jewish People. *That self-identification, which expands our spiritual horizon to embrace the whole history and destiny of our People, is as indispensable a part of our religious experience as the contemplation of Deity.*

To achieve that self-identification, the use of the Hebrew language is indispensable. It is the language that, from the beginnings of Jewish history, has helped to express and to shape the religious thought and feeling of our People. Whatever other languages they came to use in their widespread Diaspora, they always and everywhere cherished Hebrew as the *leshon hakodesh,* the sacred language of Judaism. To be sure, we want our worship to stress the universal ideals of Jewry and not be limited to its collective interests. But the use of the Hebrew language enables us, through our worship, to maintain our ties with Jewry everywhere and in every age, while leaving us free to express the most universal thoughts and sentiments.

On the other hand, we must reckon with the fact that we can hardly expect all Jews to have a knowledge of Hebrew adequate for expressing spontaneously their religious feelings and thoughts. And our questioner is right in insisting that our prayers should sincerely express our own thoughts and emotions. We would be defeating our own purpose, were we to confine the services wholly to Hebrew. They would then fail to arouse the personal emotions that evoke our faith in God. For that reason, *the principal governing the actual conduct of our worship should be to maintain a balance between the use of Hebrew and that of the vernacular.*

Mordecai M. Kaplan
Questions Jews Ask

Remember before Whom You Stand

The regulations concerning the minutiae of prayer are many: the opening treatise of the Talmud, Berachot, is entirely devoted to the subject. Schurer and other Christian theologians contend that these regulations must have stifled the whole spirit of prayer. But this is a controversial fiction; as if discipline in an army, or laws in a country, necessarily suppressed patriotism. In fact, rule and discipline in worship increase devotion: without them the noblest forms of adoration are unknown. The same is seen in the kindred realm of poetry. Elaborate schemes of metre and rhyme alone—witness the Greek poets, or Shelley, Goethe, Hugo—seem to render the highest poetry possible. With it all, none realized better than the rabbis the need for prayer to be true "service of the heart." He who prays must remember before Whom he stands, they said; and it was neither the length, nor the brevity, nor the language of the prayer that mattered, but the sincerity. "The All-merciful demands the heart" is their teaching.

Joseph H. Hertz
Daily Prayer Book

Upon Rising in the Morning

When one rises from his bed, he should not occupy himself with any mundane activity whatever. He should not even talk of anything else. He should attend to his bodily needs, wash his hands and think of the Creator of the world, focusing his thoughts on the fact that He is the One, the only unique Unity, that He is the Supreme King of kings, the Holy One, blessed be He. He is the Sovereign, the Ruler, the Source and Root of all worlds.

One should contemplate the heaven and the earth, and meditate on this verse (Isaiah 40:26): "Lift up your eyes on high and see: Who has created all these?"—meaning that He, may He be blessed, has created all from absolute non-existence, and he should think: "How abundant are Your works, O God!"

Then he should contemplate the greatness of God's works in creating the earth and all it contains—the mineral, vegetable, animal, and human kingdoms—great and wise creatures—and the wonders of the ocean and all it contains. . . . And all of these are but as a tiny seed as compared with the world of spheres . . . and all of them are as nothing in comparison with the angels . . . and all together are as non-existent in comparison with the exalted and elevated throne, and the throne is naught as compared with His Divine Glory which is the ultimate cause and ground of all existence. There is none beside Him.

Then the person will be filled with the awe and love of God, may He be blessed, and the desire to cleave to Him will enter his heart. With these thoughts let the worshiper begin his berachah: "Blessed are You O God . . ."

Isaiah Horowitz
Sha'ar Ha-Otiot, Ot Alef

If One Cries Out Many Times

A Chasid was praying with great enthusiasm, and frequently interjected the exclamation: "Father, O Father!" A second Chasid argued: "We know from the Talmud that when we obey God, He is called our Father; otherwise He is our Master. How is this Chasid so certain that he is worthy enough to call upon the Lord as his Father, not his Master?"

The Kotzker Rabbi who overheard this remark, said: "If one cries out: 'Father, O Father' many times, at last God becomes in truth his Father!"

J. K. K. Rokotz
Siach Sarfay Kodesh

"Davening" Can Become an Overwhelming Experience

Davening is not simply a manner or style of worshiping or praying. It is a much more complex experience. Like Buddhist meditation or Sufi dancing, *davening* is Judaism's central, traditional, spiritual exercise. A spiritual exercise of this type is an experience that demands one's total participation. It demands that the experiencer dive into it with a total concentration, with a directed purpose, with all doubts tucked away on a shelf for the duration of the experience. A spiritual exercise of this type is an opportunity for the conscious mind to step aside, to allow the person to shift gears into a totally different experience of reality. Practiced regularly, over time, the individual becomes transformed most deeply into one who *experiences God directly*—first, during worship, and then, later, throughout everyday life.

The daily service is my mantra. A mantra is a work, a syllable, or a sentence upon which one meditates and focuses his or her total attention. Most mantras are short, and they are recited over and over again, non-stop, for 20 minutes or more. Meditating on a mantra facilitates this spiritual transformation. *Davening* the service is reciting a 30 or 80 page mantra once. . . .

Davening is primarily a reflective, intuitive experience. It does not need to be explained, theologized, or apologized for. It can only be experienced, and the experience can become an overwhelming experience if one approaches it with an open heart.

William Blank
Journal of Reform Judaism

What Davening Is

Anyone who has *davened* (prayed) with genuinely pious Jews knows that *davening* may be conducted attentively on two levels. On one, the words of the prayer guide the attention of the worshiper; he follows the meaning and puts his heart into it. On the other level, the mood of the prayer, or rather of the occasion, takes the lead. The individual words are then transcended, their meaning is of no importance, the utterance of the lips is, as it were, a genuflexion that accompanies the devotion of the soul.

Sometimes you will hear a worshipper gabble off the words: "Blessed-aretheythatdwellin Thyhousetheyshallpraise Theeforeverselah!" He begins with a shout and trails off into a subdued drumfire of amazingly precise syllabification, right to the end of the psalm, coming up now and again with an occasional burst of intelligibility, or pausing here and there for a roulade. You would swear that the man's mind is not on the words—and it is not. Then you would add that his prayer is perfunctory, and you would more often than not be quite wrong. His soul is in the posture of prayer; he may be in the mood of supplication, of adoration, or of humility; he is using the occasion of the common gesture for a private experience; the familiar syllabic exercise is a kind of hypnotic induction. *Davening* is therefore the periodic contact with the religious emotion rather than the formal act of prayer. And the religious emotion is a daily necessity to the pious Jew.

Maurice Samuel
The World of Sholem Aleichem

The Cantor's Intent

If a cantor rejoices because he can praise God with a pleasant and beautiful voice, rejoicing with reverence, then he is praiseworthy. It is required that the one leading the service have a pleasant voice, as we find in the Talmud. . . . But if the cantor's intent is to show off his voice and be complimented for it, he is despicable. Regarding his like, it is written, "She has raised her voice against Me; therefore I hated her" (Jeremiah 12:8).

In any case, it is not correct to draw out the service. In numerous places our sages teach us to make the service brief so as not to overburden the congregation.

Shlomo ben Avraham Adret
Teshuvot Rashba

We Gain Much

When a man studies or prays with fear and love he gains much from it in that he becomes bound in his thought to the Creator, blessed be He. Such a worshiper sees nothing and hears nothing except the divine vitality that is in all things. For everything is from Him, blessed be His name; only it is clothed, as it were, in various garments. How, then, can motives of self, worldly desires, enter his mind, if all he sees before him is the vitality of the Creator alone and the spiritual delight that inheres in all things?

The Maggid of Meseritch
Esser Orot

The Flower of All Tefillah

In Tefillah you gather the strength of dedication for life, allowing this life to become the fulfillment of the Divine will, the furthering of the Divine purpose—a contribution to the success of that purpose, which God has set for humanity and Israel. Thus the flower of all Tefillah is the resolution which infuses the whole man and unites all your powers to be a servant of God in life.

Joseph Albo
Sefer Ha-Ikkarim

4 PRAYER AS PRIVILEGE AND PETITION

Pray For an End to Sin

A number of scoffers lived in Rabbi Meir's neighborhood, and they used to bother him very much. So annoyed was he that he wanted to pray that they die. His wife Beruriah said to him: "Do not pray for an end to sinners, but for an end to sin. Pray that they repent. . . ."

Rabbi Meir did so, and eventually they repented.

Berachot 10a

Thou Knowest Best

Thou knowest best what is for my good. If I recite my wants, it is not to remind Thee of them, but so that I may better understand how great is my dependence upon Thee. If, then, I ask Thee for the things that make not for my well-being, it is because I am ignorant; Thy choice is better than mine, and I submit myself to Thine unalterable decrees and Thy supreme direction.

Bachya Ibn Pakuda
Duties of the Heart

Never Cease to Seek Compassion

When Moses prayed to God that he might enter the promised land, God said, "Let it suffice thee; speak no more unto me of this matter." Yet did Moses not cease to seek compassion from God. How much less should the rest of mankind cease to keep on praying. . . .

Sifre Deuteronomy, Va'etchanen 29

When the Gates Are Closed

We are taught by our Rabbis that 'the gates of tears are not closed'; namely, that tearful pleas to God for mercy are acceptable by Him. It may be asked, since they are not closed, of what use are gates? The answer is: If one begs tearfully but without intelligence, the gates are then closed.

Medzibozer Rabbi
Butzina De-Nehorah

Forbidden Prayers

Do not pray for the impossible. Even though God has the power, do not ask Him to alter the laws of nature. . . .

It is forbidden to pray that God should do something that would change the ways of nature. . . .

Yehuda He-Chasid
Sefer Chasidim

When a Prayer of Supplication Is Legitimate

Man cannot know whether his request will be granted. This point differentiates prayer from magic. In magic man tries to force God to act in accordance with man's wishes—and he may score a visible success. But by trying to force God to do his will, man transforms Him into an idol. A god who can be forced to do man's will is an idol. The danger of magic lies in its seeming success. The successful man pays a heavy price for his achievement: he loses God. An idol can be defined as a man-made object of adoration in which the worshiper adores his own product, be it the product of his hands or the product of his mind. Idolatry is the duplication of the ego—be it the individual ego or the collective ego, as in racialism or chauvinism. Hermann Cohen once pointed out that it is no less anthropomorphic to speak of God's spirit than it is to speak of God's hands. We may commit idolatry even by speaking of God's spirit if this term denotes a concept that originates in man's mind. Authentic prayer addresses itself not to a god we make but to the God who made us. A prayer of supplication is legitimate only if man turns to God with full awareness of God's freedom of decision, prepared to accept the decision—gratefully, should it be positive, but also to accept it, though perhaps with anguish, should it be negative. God may say *yes*, but He can say *no*, too.

Ernst Simon
Tradition and Contemporary Experience

An Act of God's Love

Among God's acts of love was the fact that He gave man the opportunity to approach Him, even in this world. Even though man is immersed in darkness, and is far from the light in his natural physical state, he is still permitted to stand before God and call upon His Name. Man is thus able to temporarily elevate himself from his lowly natural state to exist in a state of closeness to God, casting his burden upon Him.

Derech Ha-Shem

He who is distressed by the tribulations of Israel and offers prayers to dispel them is permitted to complain against God.

Nachman of Bratzlav
Sefer Ha-Middot

Pray Again

Rabbi Chaninah said: If a person sees that he prays and is not answered, let him pray again. It is thus written (Psalm 27:14), "Seek God, be strong and of good courage, and seek God."

Berachot 32b

We Are Permitted to Pray to God

The Rabbi of Zans told the following story. "People come to me who ride to market every day of the week. One such man approached me and cried: 'My dear rabbi! I haven't gotten anything out of life. All week I get out of one wagon and into another. Yet when a man stops to think that he is permitted to pray to God Himself, he lacks nothing at all in the world.'"

Samuel H. Dresner
Prayer, Humility, and Compassion

The Request That Pleased The King

I heard the following parable from the Baal Shem Tov, my master: A great merciful king once announced that any request presented to him would be granted. Many people came with requests, some asking for silver, some for gold, some for high position. But there was one wise man who made a very different request. He asked the king if he could have permission to speak to him three times each day.

The king was very pleased with this unusual request, seeing that this wise man valued conversation with the king even more than gold and riches. He therefore decreed that just as this wise man shall have access to the king, so shall he have access to all the king's treasuries to take what he desires without restraint.

Jacob Joseph
Va'etchanen

Include friend and foe in your petitions, for how can one ask God for blessings which he does not want others to have?

Orchot Tzaddikim

Prayer Is the Unique Privilege of Man

God, the living God of biblical faith, does not "demand" any kind of prayer. He does not need our words of praise or adoration or petition. But *we do.* And that we can reach out to Him, address Him, and, in certain moments, find Him—this is our glory and our greatness as human beings.

Prayer is the unique, incomprehensible, and ungrounded privilege of man. The capacity to pray is one of those essentially mysterious qualities that distinguish the human species from the rest of the animal creation. That man can transcend the order of nature of which he is a part; that he can, at moments, escape the inexorable flow of time; that he can reach out of his mortal and finite being to the One who is infinite and immortal; that he can, in Martin Buber's words, address "the eternal Thou"—this is a gift of grace. It is God Himself acting.

It is something like this that the late Paul Tillich, from whom I have learned much, meant when he said that when we pray "we do something humanly impossible. We talk to somebody who is not somebody else but who is nearer to us than we ourselves are. We address somebody who can never become an object of our address because He is always subject, always acting, always creating. We tell something to Him who knows not only what we tell Him but also all the unconscious tendencies out of which our conscious words grow. This is the reason why prayer is humanly impossible. . . . It is God Himself who prays through us, when we pray to Him—God Himself in us: that is what Spirit means. Spirit is another word for 'God present,' with shaking, inspiring, transforming power. Something in us, which is not we ourselves, intercedes before God for us. We cannot bridge the gap between God and ourselves even through the most intensive and frequent prayers. The gap between God and ourselves can be bridged only by God."

Bernard Martin
An Existentialist View

Who Am I to Give Thanks to God?

The story is told of a Chasid who came to visit a famous Chasidic Rebbe, renowned as a man of prayer. On entering the prayer-room, the man found the teacher deep in thought and smoking his pipe. The man waited, then said his own prayers, and still the Rebbe did not move. Timidly the Hasid approached the master and reminded him that it would soon be past the time for praying the morning Shema. "It's all very well for a man like you," said the Rabbi; "you are satisfied to come to synagogue and say your prayers right away. But I began my prayers as soon as I rose this morning with the words: Mode Ani, 'I give thanks before Thee'; and then immediately began to meditate—'Who am I to give thanks to God?'—And I am still pondering this question."

Bernard M. Casper
Talks on Jewish Prayer

We All Stand before Him in Creaturely Needfulness

Jewish prayer covers every area of human life, the material as well as the spiritual, the personal as well as the social, the national as well as the universal. Jewish prayer shows no less appreciation of moral and spiritual values than some of the most significant tomes of the philosophers, yet a Jew prays unabashedly for his daily bread as well as for the needs of the spirit. A deep and fervent longing for the manifestation of the Divine Presence comes to expression in the prayer of the Jew, yet he will quite naturally also pray for salvation from the hands of his enemies, and see nothing incongruous in such praying. How are such apparent contradictory tendencies to be reconciled with each other? They are to be reconciled through—prayer.

The philosopher who would pray to God only for moral and spiritual goods misunderstands completely the situation in which man confronts God in prayer. Of course, there are differences between the various values of men; there are higher and lower goods, and man should always aspire to the nobler things in life. But prayer is not a dissertation on ethics; nor is it possible for a man to pray standing on ethical principles alone. As we turn to God in prayer, do we mean to make an impression on Him with the nobility of our aspirations? Do we mean to prevail upon Him by asking for the power to do good rather than for the strength to breathe and walk and work? Nothing could be more naive and less philosophical. There is indeed an order of values down here, which has meaning in relationship to man. But what is the significance of this order of human values in relationship to God? When the mystic refuses to pray for mere trifles, he should stop praying altogether. For even the noblest of man's desires, the mystical communion with God, is only a human desire and, perhaps, a mere trifle in the sight of God. Can one really maintain that a philosopher or a mystic has a greater claim to God's attention than the lowliest of His creatures? As far as our dignity is concerned in the presence of God, it is correctly summed up in a passage of Judaism's daily prayers: "Master of all worlds! It is not on account of our righteousness that we offer our supplications before Thee, but on account of Thy great compassion. What are we? What is our life? What is our goodness? What our righteousness? What our helpfulness? What our strength? What our might? What can we say in Thy Presence, Eternal One our God and God of our fathers? Indeed, all the heroes are nothing before Thee, men of renown as though they never existed, the wise as if they were without knowledge, the intelligent as though they lacked understanding; for most of their doings are worthless, and the days of their life are vain in Thy sight; man is not far above beast, for all is vanity."

That mere man should be able to confront God is logically inconceivable. Yet, it is a fact; however, not because man can approach God, but because, in His unfathomable mercy, God has approached man. Was He induced to do so by the nobility of human aspirations? What impact may all the goodness of man make on the Infinite? It is with our need alone that we may approach God in prayer. Prayer is always *T'filah L'anee,* the call of the poor. This does not mean that the one who is not an *Anee* dare not pray. Rather it indicates that we may all turn to God in prayer because each one of us stands before Him in the inescapable situation of his creaturely needfulness.

Eliezer Berkovits
Studies in Torah Judaism

Thanksgiving for the Privilege of Prayer

The ancient Rabbis had a special formula of thanksgiving for the *privilege* of prayer, and the saints availed themselves of this privilege of its full extent. Besides the obligatory prayers, the Jewish saint had his own individual prayers, some of which have come down to us. The burden of these is mostly an appeal to God's mercy for help, that He may find him worthy to do his will. "May it be Thy will," runs one of these prayers, "That we be single-hearted in the fear of Thy name; that thou remove us from all thou hatest; that thou bring us near to all thou lovest, and that thou deal with us graciously for they name's sake."

Solomon Schechter
Some Aspects of Rabbinic Theology

Prayer is a privilege. Unless we learn how to be worthy, we forfeit the right and ability to pray.

Abraham Joshua Heschel
Man's Quest for God

The Ultimate Test

Are our supplications to God heard and answered? This question takes us back to the fundamental question regarding the nature of the universe as a whole. Are they right who say "The Lord does not see it, the God of Jacob does not pay heed" (Psalm 94:7), or is there a self-evident cogency to the argument "Shall He who implants the ear not hear, He who forms the eye not see?" (Psalm 94:9)? But even assuming that He does "hear" and "see," is He *concerned,* and does He respond in accordance with the standards of justice and mercy?

We do not *know,* and we cannot possibly ever know, the answer to these questions. We either believe that "more things are wrought by prayer than this world dreams of"—and that God hears the cry of the stranger, the widow, and the fatherless who are wronged and afflicted, and responds to their cry (Exodus 22:20–23), and that "The Lord is near to all who call upon Him, to all who call Him with sincerity" (Psalm 145:18)—or we do not. No amount of "proof" can validate either position beyond a reasonable doubt, nor even establish a reasonable preponderance of proof in favor of the one position over the other.

But there are some things that we know about prayer with a certainty that is at least as great, if not greater, than the certainty with which we know the phenomena brought to our attention by our five senses. We "know" in the innermost recesses of our being that without the belief that God "hears" and "responds" to our prayers, prayer addressed to God makes no sense. We know, moreover, that the thoughtful recitation of our needs before God makes us keenly aware of both how much their fulfillment depends upon our own efforts, and how greatly dependent we are for their fulfillment upon our fellow men and upon factors that are unknown to us.

We know that the ability and the privilege of reciting our needs before God is our ultimate defense against being overwhelmed by utter despair. For we would not have uttered the prayer at all if it were not for a glimmer of hope that moves us to do so. And we know from the testimony of others, and many of us from our own experience, that the heartfelt utterance of a prayer can ignite that glimmer into a flame that brightens, at least for a moment, the darkness which surrounds us.

In that moment of illumination, we may see with persuasive clarity that God owes us nothing, that "His thoughts are not our thoughts" (Isaiah 58:8), that what we may be praying for may not be to our advantage, and that He has ways of exercising His love, justice, and mercy which are beyond our knowledge or power to comprehend. In such a moment of illumination, we may see that to love God means, among other things, to subdue our will to His, so that we accept what we deem to be His favorable response to our supplications without self-righteousness, and what to us may appear as His unfavorable response without resentment. For the ultimate test of whether our prayers have or have not been answered is whether we rise from them reinvigorated in our belief that life is good and more firmly committed to living the good life. All else is of secondary importance.

Simon Greenberg
A Jewish Philosophy and Pattern of Life

Not Everyone's Requests Should Be Granted

There was a case where Rabban Gamliel went to Rabbi Chelbo in Keruyah. He said to him, "Pray for me." He responded, "May God give you as your heart desires" (Psalm 20:5).

Rav Huna, son of Rabbi Yitzchak, said: This is not what he told him. Rather he said, "God should fill all your requests" (Psalm 20:6). He said to him, "This is a prayer that one should not say to every man. Why? Sometimes in a person's heart lurks the intent to steal or to sin, or do evil, which is not fitting for him. How can one say to him 'May God give you as your heart desires'? But because Rabban Gamliel's heart was perfect with his Creator, he said such a prayer for him."

Midrash Tehillim 20:9

I Pray That I May Give Myself to God

Who will presume to speak of futility in the role of spirit, who will say that aspiration is unavailing because it seems to be what the world calls futile? How can prayer be futile, for through prayer one reaches out—as is possible in no other way—into the life of another, one reaches out into the life of all. Prayer might almost be defined as the mingling of the stream of life of the individual with the seas of infinite life; the stream of the soul is not lost or spent, but regained and enriched through commingling with the tides of life, infinite and eternal. . . .

I pray not that I may have, but that I may be. I pray not that God may give me, but that I may give myself to God. Nor shall I cease to pray when God withholds from me, for from men God may not withhold the infinite and eternal of themselves. Prayer is the joy, high and unutterable, of the soul's outreaching to Him who is the Soul of Souls.

Stephen S. Wise
Religion

Rabbi Yochanan and Rabbi Elazar both said: Even if a sword is on your neck do not desist from praying for mercy.

Berachot 10a

An Opportunity to Approach God

Among God's acts of love was the fact that He gave man the opportunities to approach Him, even in this physical world. Even though man is immersed in darkness and is far from the Light in his natural physical state, he is still permitted to stand before God and call upon His name. Man is thus able temporarily to elevate himself from his lowly natural state to exist in a state of closeness to God, casting his burden on Him.

Moshe Chaim Luzzatto
Mesillat Yesharim

Overcoming Barriers

Prayer serves to sow in the heart of one who prays a dependence on the Lord and a need for attachment to Him; and when man has attained an understanding and recognition of his complete dependence upon his Creator for the very fact of his being alive, and for all his requirements and needs, and the realisation of it spreads as a living emotion through his heart, then will he overcome all inhibitions and barriers, turn towards God and see himself standing before Him.

Haim Hamiel
Prayer

What to Ask For

When you pray for your needs, your intent should not be that God give you riches, honors and physical enjoyment. Rather, ask that God give you your needs so that you should be better able to serve Him.

Judah Löw
Gevurot Ha-Shem

Sincerity of Heart

There was a herdsman who was in the habit of saying every day: "Lord of the world, You know well that if You had cattle and gave them to me to tend, I would take no wages from You because I love You."

Once a learned man, who chanced to hear this prayer, said: "Fool, do not pray in this manner!" When the herdsman asked: "How, then, should I pray?" the learned man taught him the traditional blessings, the reading of the *Shema* and the *Amidah*. But, when the learned man had left, the herdsman forgot all that he had been taught and did not pray at all. He was afraid to say his old prayer because the saintly man had warned him against it.

In a dream by night, the learned man heard a voice saying: "If you do not tell him to say what he was accustomed to say before you met him, misfortune shall befall you, since you have deprived God of one who belongs to the future world."

The learned man at once went to the herdsman and told him what he had dreamed, adding: "Continue to say what you used to say. The Merciful One desires sincerity of heart."

Yehuda He-Chasid
Sefer Chasidim

We Stand in Prayer with Needs and Responsibilities

Two opposing views are often voiced regarding such petitionary prayer. Some feel that requests of a personal nature belong to an earlier, more primitive stage of religion and have no place in modern worship. Others hold that petitions are meaningful only if we believe that they will be "granted," in a direct, immediate, literal sense. Reflection would reveal that both of the above views are too narrow to embrace the full meaning of prayer.

If the religious dimension is to be maintained amid the actual pressures of life, then its high moments must be integrated with the harsh realities of human existence. Religious contemplation and worship must not become an ethereal domain of solitary and timeless reflection, insulated from the burdens of daily existence. Hence, the supreme importance of including our personal needs, in all their paltriness, within the perspective of our yearning to become part of His design. It is not as a disembodied soul that man stands in prayer, but as a living human being, with needs and responsibilities. The individual also remains mindful that wholeness in prayer encompasses a selfhood not detached from his community seeking the God of the universe.

The consummation of self-surrender in prayer is made more meaningful when we bring to mind the many ways in which the divine image is imprisoned within us. Religion is the cutting edge of the soul as it seeks reality; man's soul is, at the same time, the reflection of his feeble, earth-bound personality.

To go from the contemplation of the divine to concern with personal needs is not anti-climactic. On the contrary, it is the only way to make religion meaningful. The individual, frail and sinful though he be, is yet the purpose of all creation. The divine image is reflected not in the "soul of the world," but in the soul of man. Boundless and eternal as is the cosmos, the soul of man is closer to the Supreme Being than the universe with its billions of galaxies.

In the Jewish faith the concrete individual mirrors the divine being. In primitive societies and totalitarian countries the individual is submerged by the mass, but in Scriptures he is the supreme concern of the Almighty. Abraham arises to defy the entire pagan world. Jeremiah is made into "a fortified wall" and a "pillar of brass" that would resist the surging mob.

Moses is told that God prefers him to all the children of Israel. A great Chasidic teacher said that a person should always bear two verses in mind: "It is for my sake that the world was created" and "I am but dust and ashes."

If the individual is of supreme importance, the worshiper may well feel that his efforts to deal with his problems and concerns form part of the movement of the world toward the perfection of the "Kingdom of Heaven." As Hillel put it, "If I am not for myself, who will be for me? But if I am for myself only, what am I?" (Ethics of the Fathers 1:14).

A person should see his own needs in the light of his overriding concern for self-fulfillment, and understand that the fulfillment of his self is attained through his integration within the purpose and design of God.

Jacob B. Agus
Great Jewish Ideas

We Cannot Do without Needful Sustenance

We may pray not on account of what we are, but rather on account of what we lack. It is, therefore, not the spiritual quality of the good that we ask for which matters, not the philosophical depth of our thought nor the mystical surrender of our personal desires, but the intensity of the need, the depth of the misery alone out of which we call Him who is near because He is needed. One can pray only because God does not despise "a broken and oppressed heart." At best, the plea of the philosopher or the mystic will be prayer; but no more prayer than the cry that reaches God in the dead of night out of the dungeons of a soul along skid row. In fact, the philosopher who would pray to God only for the nobler things of life may easily be a pedantic bore, imagining that God might be impressed with his ethics but not with the hunger pangs of his poor ulcerated bowels. And how amused might God be—or perhaps, disgusted?—by the antics of the little mystic who would "ask of God as a gift God himself," and would consider it below the dignity of his faith to settle for anything less, but yet would ask for the first prize in the religious lottery with the same greediness of the soul with which the next best yokel may hope for divine assistance in order to hit the jackpot in the Irish sweepstakes. It is unlikely that God could be moved by the one more than by the other. It is not our greatness—which counts for nothing in His eyes—that causes Him to make Himself accessible to human entreaty, but His fatherly compassion with the lowliness of our creaturely situation. A form of mystical communion with God may indeed be God's greatest gift to man. But man can live without the enjoyment of the glory of the Presence; he cannot do without his needful sustenance. On account of that alone may he pray.

Eliezer Berkovits
Studies in Torah Judaism

What Shall We Pray For?

What shall we pray for? For bicycles, convertibles, dividends? We have not been taught so to pray. Our prayer book teaches us to ask for forgiveness or knowledge of God's law, for purity of heart, for those qualities and those spiritual insights which enable us to see God's will clearly and to pray as did Eliezer ben Hyrcanus, Talmudic sage, hundreds of years ago: "Do Thy will in Heaven and give composure of spirit to those who worship Thee on earth." Prayer's purpose is not to change nature but human nature; not to ask God to break His laws, but to help us keep His laws.

I do not know whether prayer will bring rain to a drought-stricken Texas. But I do know that prayer will bring rain into a dried-up heart, warmth into a cold soul, calm into a stormy spirit. We come to God as a child does to his parents to pour out our troubles and find in His presence the courage to carry on. I have had the experience, you have too, of coming into a house of worship with all the ache and weariness of heart that we can bear—and then, in God's presence, leafing through the pages of the prayer book, hearing the music of religious yearning, and feeling the ache and the weariness and the pain fade away and new courage and new hope come to replace them.

Robert I. Kahn
Lessons for Life

What Commences in Petition Concludes in Prayer

There are numerous prayers of petition in our prayer books. They are, we should note, however, put into the plural tense, so that we are taught to pray as a member of the community of Israel: "Hear *our* cry; forgive *us*; heal *us*; blow the great horn of *our* freedom." It is as if we were being told that we should really not pray for our own needs; that is not true prayer; often it is only selfish concern. Our prayers should be for His will to be done, for our wills to bend to His, for Him to enter our hearts. Yet, we are human and have human needs and desires that stir us deeply. And it is easier for us to ask for our own needs than for God's, for our will to be done rather than for His. Therefore, we may ask and we may petition. But we are not to ask for ourselves. We are to ask for our people and all mankind. And, then, in the midst of this asking and petitioning, we will come to understand that all our petitions, all our requests, all our pleas are only so that we might turn away from the world and stand before Him for a moment to know His love and strength; that His presence might be made manifest to us.

What begins with man's request ends with God's presence; what starts in the narrowness of the ego, emerges into the wide expanse of humanity; what originates in concern for the self becomes a concern for others and concern for God's concern; what commences in petition concludes as prayer.

Samuel H. Dresner
Prayer, Humility, and Compassion

God's Responsiveness to Men's Prayers

Unselfishness in petitionary prayer was strongly urged by the rabbis, and this was one of the major reasons for their preference for public over private prayer. They frequently admonished men to pray for one another: "A prayer on behalf of another is answered first"; "He who misses the opportunity of praying for another is called a sinner"; "Elimelech and his sons [who, according to the Book of Ruth, left Palestine for Moab and thus, according to the rabbis, did not pray for their famine-stricken brethren] were punished for failing to pray for their generation" (Bava Kama 92a; Bava Batra 91b). The concern for the welfare of the total community is particularly manifest in their rather strange prayer, "Let not the prayer of wayfarers find entrance, O Lord, before Thee." This because wayfarers would be inclined selfishly to ask for fine weather when the general good required rain.

Petitionary prayer, furthermore, must not be a substitute for human effort. The rabbis cite the example of the Israelites at the Red Sea cowering before the approaching Egyptian hosts. Though they and their leader Moses cried to God in their extremity, the Midrash (Exodus Rabbah 21:10) declares that the sea was divided for them only after Israel had stepped into it and the waters had reached their noses. Man must first do to the utmost what lies in his power; only then may he properly call for a manifestation of the power that transcends his own.

Above all, petitionary prayer, according to Jewish tradition, must in every case be uttered in the spirit of ultimate resignation to God's will and acceptance of God's sovereignty. Rabbi Eliezer said: "Thus shall a man pray: 'Do Thy will, O God, in heaven above and bestow tranquillity of spirit on those who fear Thee below, and what is good in Thine own sight do. Blessed art Thou, O Lord, who hearest prayer'" (Berachot 29b).

To accept God's will emphatically does not mean for classical Judaism, however, that God is impassive or unresponsive to human supplications. The great Jewish teachers of the past rejected the conception of God that lies behind the speech John Milton puts into Adam's mouth in *Paradise Lost:*

> . . . if by prayer
> Incessant I could hope to change the will
> Of him who all things can, I would not cease
> To weary him with my assiduous cries:
> But prayer against his absolute decree
> No more avails than breath against the wind,
> Blown stifling back on him that breathes it forth;
> Therefore to his great bidding I submit.

Such a conception of God and the idea that "battering the gates of heaven with storms of prayer" is a futile exercise may be congenial to the modern temperament. Jewish tradition, however, acknowledges both the sovereignty of God's will and his responsiveness to men's prayers.

Bernard Martin
Prayer in Judaism

God's Gardeners

How does so lowly a creature as man
  dare to come before God
  three times a day
  to seek fulfillment of his needs?

There was a king who had a garden
  in which he took great pride.
He hired a certain man to care for it:
  to plant, to trim, to cultivate the earth.
Now that gardener needed sustenance for himself
  and various supplies to tend the royal garden.
Should he be ashamed to come before the king
  each day and seek that which he needs?
It is for the king himself that he is working!

But such is not the case for a lazy worker,
  one who does nothing for the garden,
  but only takes what is given him
  to satisfy his gluttonous desires.
How can he dare to come again before the king and
  say:
  "Give me what I want"?

Divrat Shelomo 2:50b–51a
Arthur Green
Barry Holtz
Your Word Is Fire

Three Advantages of Petitionary Prayers

Basically, there are three main advantages in availing ourselves of the petitionary prayers furnished by the Tradition:—

(a) There is, first of all, the recognition of our dependence upon God. We are not alone in the world. Our limited human strength is not the only power which gets things accomplished. With the help of God, goals can be reached which would otherwise be beyond us. Petitionary prayer makes us aware of this.

(b) Petitionary prayer, sanctioned by Tradition, also gives us the confidence that what we are asking for is in consonance with the teachings of our religion. We do not pray for the attainment of goals which would be contrary to the aims of our faith or irreconcilable with the nature of God as Judaism conceives of Him. Consequently, knowing that what we express in prayer is acceptable to God, we can feel all the more assured of divine help in the attainment of our verbalized goals.

(c) Petitionary prayer, sanctioned by Tradition, enlarges the range of our concerns. People can become very egotistical and self-centered in prayer. They can confine their prayers to their own very immediate concerns, paying little attention, if any, to the needs and the concerns of their fellowmen. But a petitionary prayer, uttered by a whole community, can save us from such pitfalls.

Jakob J. Petuchowski
Dynamics and Doctrine

Be Careful when Praying

It is essential that you know how to be careful when you make supplication for your needs. God forbid that your intention should be for the gratification of your own desires, for this is self-worship, of which God has no desire, indeed it is abhorrent in His eyes. . . . Therefore, when a man asks God for his material needs, such as health, riches, peace, and other material perfections, his intention should be that these will help him to serve his Creator, seeing that a man cannot properly serve God if he lacks the material goods of life, which are God-given aids for the aim he really desires—the improvement of the soul.

Jacob Emden
Jewish Prayer

We Need to Pray for Our Own Sakes

Prayer influences not God, but ourselves. He does not need our worship. Our wants our yearnings, our lightest thoughts are known to Him as soon as they are known to us. It is for our own sakes that we need to pray. It is a need far greater than the trivial wants that form the burden of many of our petitions. We too often pray for little, even for worthless things, for favors that are more than doubtful. But what we most need, though we do not always see it, is the help that comes from prayer itself—help to bear our load more bravely, to face temptation more resolutely. We need to get the very mood of surrender, to realize that we are but as little children in the hands of a loving, yet infinitely wise Parent, humble servants of an august Master. And, therefore, even when our prayers seem to fail, they succeed; for they effect that spiritual uplifting which is far more worth having than the things we pray for.

Morris Joseph
Judaism as Creed and Life

"No" Is Also an Answer

It is in the nature of any discussion of petitionary prayer that the question arises whether God "answers" prayer. An unequivocally affirmative answer is given to this question both in the Bible and in Rabbinic literature. But just as unequivocal is the testimony of those who have prayed and have then found that their petitions have not been granted. It all depends on how one looks upon petitionary prayer and upon—God.

After all, it would be a rather primitive concept of God if one were to regard Him as a kind of cosmic vending machine. You insert a prayer, and out comes whatever boon you have selected! This is not to say that such concepts of God and of prayer have never been held within the confines of Judaism. But such popular notions of prayer do not represent Judaism's most mature thought on this subject.

The view which sees prayer as "answered" only when the specific good we have requested is actually granted is a view which leaves out of account the kind of sentiment voiced in the "emergency prayers." . . . One of those prayers expressed the thought that, while the needs of Israel were many, Israel's understanding in formulating them was limited. Another prayer, that of Rabbi Eliezer, asked God to do that which is good in His own sight. Clearly, there is a recognition here of the fact that, while God *is* concerned with man's highest good, man's formulation of what he, man, *thinks* is his highest good is not necessarily always adequate. Man, in fact, may voice requests which, in the long run, are *not* for his own good. If God were to grant such requests, then He would not really be concerned with man's true welfare.

Put differently, the same thought may be expressed by saying that God's "answer" to man's prayer need not invariably be an affirmative answer. God must also be thought capable of saying "No!" Perhaps this is indeed the major difference between engaging in magic and engaging in prayer. Magic, by definition, *must* work. If it does not yield results, then, in the view of the practitioner of magic, something must have gone wrong with the performance of the magical rite; and he will repeat the rite in a more careful and meticulous manner. Prayer, on the other hand, is addressed to a God who has a will and a mind of His own. God cannot be manipulated by man. He can only be *addressed*. He may or may not grant a specific request. But there is no mechanism of man's devising which would compel Him to do so. In addressing God, man knows that a "No" can be as much of an "answer" as a "Yes."

Jakob J. Petuchowski
Dynamics and Doctrine

When a man's heart is heavy and full of anxiety, he can lighten it through ardent prayer and a belief in God's mercies.

Rabbi Bunam
Maasiyot Noraim

5 GIVING THANKS AND PRAISE

Lord, I thank Thee for the goodness of growth, I thank Thee for the slice of bread and the prayerful mood.

Ben Amittai
quoted by S. Halkin in
Modern Hebrew Literature

Only God May We Serve and Praise

God is the only one whom we may serve and praise. Only His greatness may we sing, and only His commandments may we obey.

We may not act in this manner toward anything beneath Him, whether it be an angel, a star, one of the elements, or any combination of them. All these have a predetermined nature; therefore none can have authority or free will. Only God has these attributes.

It is not proper to serve these things or to make them intermediaries to bring us closer to God. All our thoughts should be directed only toward Him, and nothing else should even be considered.

This principle forbids all forms of idolatry, and it constitutes a major portion of the Torah.

Moses Maimonides
Commentary on Mishnah, Sanhedrin 10:1

Brethren, give me a God, for I am full of prayer!

David Frishman
Hayadata? Kol Kitvay

Garlands for God

An angel collects all the prayers offered in the synagogues, weaves them into garlands, and puts them on God's head.

Rabbi Meir
Exodus Rabbah

Praise . . . in All Jewish Prayer

"Praised be Thou, O God . . ." is the basic prayer in Judaism: There is no prayer in which, implicitly or explicitly, praise is not an essential element. A Jew recites a berachah over bread, wine, other kinds of food; on first seeing a tree or animal of a species previously unknown to him; on seeing the ocean and a rainbow. He recites one beracha when he sees a great Jewish sage, and another when he sees a great Gentile one; one on hearing good news and another on hearing bad news. And a series of early morning berachot ends with one that discloses the root of praise and hence of prayer itself. "Praised be Thou, Lord our God, King of the world, who removest sleep from my eyes and slumber from my eyelids." A Jew awakens and is astonished and grateful: He is both because sleep has not been death. The Creation is renewed, every day.

Praise is implicit or explicit in all Jewish prayer.

Emil L. Fackenheim
What Is Judaism?

Why We Praise Him

Why should we praise God? And why should we thank Him? Is He not above our thanks and praises? Aristotle, in a passage which probably refers to Plato, said that "everybody may criticize him; but who is permitted to praise him?" And Goethe expressed the same concern when he said, *Wer einen lobt, stellt sich ihm gleich,* "He who praises another person places himself on the other's level." If there are valid doubts about our moral right to praise other human beings, must our doubts not be much more severe in our relationship with God? Why then do we praise or thank Him?

We praise God because our hearts need to praise Him. Once, when my son was four years old, he happened to see some beautiful flowers and said to me: "Abba, I am happy with these flowers. What is the proper benediction for them?" Though a small child, he expressed a universal human sentiment. Children can love and enjoy flowers just as deeply as adults can, perhaps even more so. But this child was a little Jew who had already learned in his parents' home that nothing is eaten or experienced without a berachah, a benediction. Hence it was natural for him to seek a specific Jewish religious formulation to express a general human emotion.

Prayer and religious observance must, of course, be more than merely the products of a conditioning process in the home of one's parents. They must be rooted in a deeply felt and affirmed conviction—a conviction expressed, for instance, in a beautiful saying of the Talmud, "He who enjoys anything of this world without a benediction is likened to a man who robs the sanctuary." The Talmud Yerushalmi makes the point even more strongly when it says that a berachah is the price we pay for being permitted to enjoy this world. To thank God and to praise Him is our acknowledgment that God is our Creator and the Creator of the universe.

Ernst Simon

Tradition and Contemporary Experience

Trivial Acts—Supreme Miracles

The sense of the "miracles which are daily with us," the sense for the "continual marvels," is the source of prayer. There is no worship, no music, no love, if we take for granted the blessings or defeats of living. No routine of the social, physical, or physiological order must dull our sense of surprise at the fact that there *is* a social, a physical, or a physiological order. We are trained in maintaining our sense of wonder by uttering a prayer before the enjoyment of food. Each time we are about to drink a glass of water, we remind ourselves of the eternal mystery of creation, "Blessed be Thou . . . by Whose word all things come into being." A trivial act and a reference to the supreme miracle. Wishing to eat bread or fruit, to enjoy a pleasant fragrance or a cup of wine; on tasting fruit in season for the first time; on seeing a rainbow, or the ocean; on noticing trees when they blossom; on meeting a sage in Torah or in secular learning; on hearing good or bad tidings—we are taught to invoke His great name and our awareness of Him. Even on performing a physiological function we say "Blessed be Thou . . . who healest all flesh and *doest wonders.*"

This is one of the goals of the Jewish way of living: to experience commonplace deeds as spiritual adventures, to feel the hidden love and wisdom in all things.

Abraham Joshua Heschel
God in Search of Man

This was the purpose of the whole creation, that man should recognize and know Him and give praise to His name.

Nachmanides
quoted by Solomon Schechter in
Studies in Judaism

When There Is Nothing to Hope For

There are times when the gates of prayer seem to be closed, when even the prayers of the *Tsadikim* are powerless, times when all seems to be lost, when the doom impending becomes the doom inevitable, when the evil decreed becomes reality.

It is one of the rules of Jewish prayer, that "man is obligated to bless God for the evil that befalls him as well as for the good that he receives." The insight on which this concept is based is derived from the words of the Bible: "And thou shalt love the Eternal One, thy God with all thine heart, and with all thy soul, and with all thy might." The phrase "with *all* thy soul" is interpreted as meaning, "even if He takes your soul." The Jew does not minimize the evil and call it good. Evil is evil and good is good; and sorrow is not joy and joy is not sorrow. Does he then submit? Submission is an attitude of passivity; the service of God is the supreme human activity. There can be no human situation which is exempted from the service of the heart. In this service, at times, the heart itself may be required. At such moments, there is of course no room for supplication. All has been said; the case is closed and there is nothing to ask for. Is this the end of the confrontation, the end of prayer? On the contrary; when there is nothing to hope for, one hopes for God alone. When there is nothing to expect, one deals with God alone. It is then that the confrontation between God and man reaches its ultimate culmination. One may still make Him the confidant of one's sorrow, but instead of importuning, one accepts; instead of pleading, one praises.

Jews through the ages have incorporated this aspect of prayer in their lives. Whenever the heavy hand of destiny strikes irrevocably, the Jew stands up and prays, not for himself but for the sanctification of God's name and the establishment of His kingdom: *Yitgaddal v'Yitkaddash Shmeh Rabba,* "Magnified and sanctified be His name in the world which He has created according to His will." However, no people on earth have practiced this kind of prayer as the Jews have on the numberless occasions of darkest martyrdom. When there was nothing to hope for, God was sufficient unto their untold millions. The prayers of Jewish martyrdom have been God's greatest triumph with man and man's incomparable triumph over the world.

Eliezer Berkovits
Studies in Torah Judaism

To Be Spiritually Alive

The words of the Midrash sound constantly in my ears: "The wicked is as one dead, even in his lifetime, for he sees the sun rise without reciting the blessing 'Thou who formest light,' he sees its setting without reciting the blessing 'Who bringest on the evening twilight'; he eats and drinks without thanking God. But the righteous thank God for whatever they eat and drink and see and hear." What does the Midrash mean? Surely the mere recitation of "Thou who formest Light" and "Who bringest on the evening twilight" cannot infuse life into the righteous any more than the failure to recite them can deprive the wicked of life so that he should be "as one dead." The meaning of the Midrash is that the wicked is so dead spiritually that he cannot feel the need to recite the benediction and take delight in so doing; he is so dead that he cannot sense the mystery in the rising and setting of the sun, in the piece of bread that he eats and the measure of water that he drinks; he is unaware of the eternal link between these things and the whole of existence and with God who dwells in this existence. The wicked is as one dead because he has lost the sense of wonder, because he views the appearances of eternity as mundane happenings.

Hayim Greenberg
The Inner Eye

Why Praise God?

Why then praise God? What is the purpose of such praise? One of the reasons is that it is in this way that our minds are directed to higher ideals. By speaking of God as merciful, compassionate and just, man reminds himself that these qualities are worth making his own, that if he is to be God-like—and the imitation of God is the religious ideal—then he too must practice these virtues. The statement: "God is merciful" implies a belief that the universe is so constructed that compassion and kindliness and pity are absolute values and that for man to be in tune with life, at peace with the world and at peace with himself, he must cultivate these values. That the cruel and unfeeling and ungenerous person is a misfit out of tune with ultimate reality.

It goes deeper than this. God exists, but unless man recognizes His existence and unless belief in His existence has some influence on man's life and character, then God does not exist for man. What is the meaning of the grand old Jewish doctrine of Kiddush Hashem, the Sanctification of God's Name, if not this, that God only exists for man when man recognizes His sovereignty? The Sages had their own way of expressing this idea that, in a sense, God depends upon man, just as man depends upon God. In the Pesikta of Rab Kahana, an ancient rabbinic Midrash, we read: "Ye are my witnesses, the Eternal speaks, and I am God"; Rabbi Simeon ben Yohai said: "If ye give witness unto me, then I am the Eternal. If ye be not my witnesses, then I am not the Eternal, as it were."

Louis Jacobs
Jewish Prayer

In Prayer We Praise

In prayer we praise. Standing in His presence and opening our eyes to His wonders both in the world of nature and the world of man, viewing the majesty of the heavens and the innocence of a child, knowing the fragrance of a flower and the warmth of a friend's hand, gazing upon a distant mountain and a deed of kindness, watching a bird in its flight and a baby smile, experiencing the cool breeze of a summer wind and the warm love of one's beloved, feeling all the beauty and goodness and grandeur of the world—we give praise and thanksgiving unto Him who formed the earth and breathed the breath of life into man, by whose word all was brought forth, Who looked out upon creation and said it was good, even very good, and by whose goodness and mercy the miracles of creation are renewed each day.

Bless the Lord Oh my soul.
O Lord my God Thou art very great,
Thou art clothed with honour and majesty.
O Lord how manifold are Thy works
In wisdom hast Thou made them all.
O Lord how excellent is Thy name in all the
earth.

Samuel H. Dresner
Prayer, Humility, and Compassion

Even from the mud, I will sing unto Thee, my God, even from the mud.

Jacob Glatstein
Von Yash Iz Gekumen

Why Not?

One who crosses the ocean and is rescued from a shipwreck gives thanks unto the Lord. But why should we not thank God if we cross without a mishap? One who is cured of a dangerous illness blesses the Lord. Why should we not bless Him, when He grants us health and preserves us from illness?

The Radziminer Rebbe
Maasiyot Noraim

God is not dependent on being glorified by His creatures. . . . But all creatures justify their creation by honoring the Lord.

Judah Löw
From the World of Cabbalah

When We See Beautiful Trees

Rabbi Judah declared:

In the spring when a man goes forth and sees beautiful trees swaying in the air, he should stop and offer a prayer: "Blessed is the Lord for having created a world in which nothing is wanting and for having fashioned living things and beautiful trees and plants to delight the heart of man."

Berachot 43b

He who has God for his heritage should bless and praise Him, since this is the only reward he can offer.

Philo
Sobriety

What Every Author Desires

God created man to admire the splendor of the world. Every author, be he ever so great, desires the praise of his work.

Heinrich Heine
Harzreise

The Difference between Prayer and Worship

I am a firm believer in public worship.
I want to hold and read the liturgy of my people.
The worship that I love is something finer and wiser than prayer.
Prayer begins in need.
Worship begins in reverence.
Prayer is a measure of man's anxiety. Worship is the measure of man's commitment.
Prayer begins in the overheated heart. Worship begins in the reflective soul.
Prayer is half-formed—a thing of the moment. Worship is sculptured—a thing of beauty.
Prayer is an urgency. Worship is a discipline.
We pray when life is too much for us. We worship, the better to live.

Daniel Jeremy Silver
CCAR Journal

Why We Thank

As to the thanksgiving prayer itself, we do not thank for a specific blessing but for God's miracles that are with us every day and for His benefits that we receive at all times, "evening, morning and noon." We thank Him, for He is "the Good One whose mercy never ceases," because He is "the Merciful One whose loving-kindness never ends." Here, thanksgiving has obviously become only another version of praise. However, just as supplication anticipates thanksgiving, so does thanksgiving hint at supplication. Since thanksgiving here is not a spontaneous response to a unique experience of having dramatically received a divine blessing but is tied to the normal routine of our everyday existence, how does one know that there is really occasion for giving thanks? How do we know of the miracles and benefits of God which are always with us? The Jewish answer is that one knows it because one lives, because man's dependence on God is such that he could not live for one moment without the goodness and mercy of God. We thank because we realize in the needfulness of our nature that we could not exist for a single breath without the Merciful One whose loving-kindness never ceases. Since every moment of man's life is a three-fold occasion, for praise, supplication, and thanksgiving, the three types of prayer have been woven into one pattern. The theme of each one of them becomes meaningful in the context of the other two. We praise, almost thanking, with a hint of supplication; we supplicate and yet worship with anticipation of thanksgiving; we thank with praises for being sustained ceaselessly.

Eliezer Berkovits
Studies in Torah Judaism

The universe throbs with Thy pauseless praise.

Eliezer Hakalir
The Lord Is King

Gratefulness Makes the Soul Great

To pray is to take notice of the wonder, to regain a sense of the mystery that animates all beings, the divine margin in all attainments. Prayer is our humble answer to the inconceivable surprise of living. It is all we can offer in return for the mystery by which we live. Who is worthy to be present at the constant unfolding of time? Amidst the meditation of mountains, the humility of flowers—wiser than all alphabets—clouds that die constantly for the sake of His glory, we are hating, hunting, hurting. Suddenly we feel ashamed of our clashes and complaints in the face of the tacit glory in nature. It is so embarrassing to live! How strange we are in the world, and how presumptuous our doings! Only one response can maintain us: gratefulness for witnessing the wonder, for the gift of our unearned right to serve, to adore, and to fulfill. It is gratefulness which makes the soul great.

Abraham Joshua Heschel
Man's Quest for God

"They shall declare My glory among the nations."

What is His glory? That His children declare His glory among the nations.

Eleazar ben Pedat
Midrash Tehillim

Our Humanity—A Gift Given out of Love

Every human being is in some degree an artist, a scientist, and a moralist. His talents in these areas of creative activity may be sharply limited or they may be remarkably productive, but no normal man is without some concern for the values of truth, beauty and goodness. No normal man is utterly bereft of the capacity to love. How did we get that way? What did we do to deserve the talents and the capacities which make us human?

The very formulation of the question prepares us for the answer. *The shattering truth is that we do not deserve them at all and that we could not possibly deserve them.*

Nobody ever earned the right to be able to love. No person ever earned the right to be able to write a poem, compose a symphony, or paint a picture—even badly. No human being ever earned the right to be able to have a concern for his fellow man and the corresponding need to create the kind of society in which that concern could be fulfilled. We earn none of these things. Our human talents come to us not as of right, *but as gifts—as gifts freely given, not as rewards earned.* Which is to say that no human being ever deserved to be human, if by "deserve" we mean that the record somehow establishes our claim to those creative talents that distinguish man from the rest of the known universe. A man's humanity is not the payment of a debt; it is a gift given out of love. This may well be one of the profounder meanings of the Biblical statement, "And God created man in His own image." God graciously, lovingly permitted us to be creators too.

The consciousness that we are loved with a love that prompts such magnificent gifts, with a love so abiding and unfailing that it never withdraws its gifts, inevitably invokes the response that all love and all gifts evoke: the response of gratitude. The expression of that gratitude is prayer.

Dudley Weinberg
The Efficacy of Prayer

Prayer—Grateful Communion with the Infinite

The fact that even the petitions are also praises of God and, therefore, not exclusively or even predominantly petitional in mood, clearly reveals a significant attitude toward prayer itself as a spiritual exercise. This attitude has been specifically stated in the following rabbinic statement: "A man should always utter the praises of God before he offers his petitions" (Berachot 32a). Judging by this mood in the *T'filo*, prayer is primarily the achievement of an affirmative relationship to God, a sense of gratitude and appreciation for the blessings we have received. If our faith can succeed in curing us of the mood of constant discontent and can teach us to find joyous gratitude in whatever happiness we already have, however small it may be, then it will engender a healthy-mindedness within us that makes for a happy life, itself the answer to most of our prayers. This habit of praising God rather than begging from Him has become, through centuries of this type of prayer, a prevalent state of mind which enabled our fathers to find joy even in minor blessings and thus played its part in preserving Israel through the vicissitudes of history. A poverty-stricken, forlorn, exiled Jew, raising his last crust of bread to his mouth, might perhaps be justified in cursing his lot and denouncing God, but instead it would not enter his mind to partake of this bit of bread without first saying, "Praised be Thou O Lord Who bringest forth food from the earth." The rabbis speak even of a higher state of heroism, a more triumphant conquest of bitterness when they say, "A man should praise God even for misfortunes as much as he praises Him for happiness" (Yerushalmi, Berachot 9:5). Whether this lofty courage is attainable by the average Jew or not, he learns to feel and to express, or perhaps to express and thus to feel, a constant sense of gratitude to the Master of the Universe. Prayer in Israel teaches man to overcome bitterness and self-pity; to think not of what the world owes *him,* but what he owes the world and God. It is not primarily piteous pleading but is essentially grateful communion with the Infinite.

Solomon B. Freehof
The Small Sanctuary

Thanksgiving Makes Us Conscious of Our Blessings

One of the most characteristic goals of religion is the building of a *discipline of thanksgiving.* To this end, Judaism, for example, has created an all-encompassing system of benedictions which it enjoins upon its devotees. Upon partaking of bread or wine, donning a new garment, inhaling a fragrance, experiencing the majesty of a storm, beholding a beautiful woman or a great sage, man is called upon to pronounce a blessing in praise of the King of the Universe, who has thus manifested His goodness and creative powers. The expression of thanksgiving is essential not to the giver, but to the recipient of the gift, because it makes him conscious of the blessings which he enjoys and heightens his delight in these gifts when they are present.

This discipline of thanksgiving in human life proves at least equally valuable when the blessings are lacking. When need or failure, illness or bereavement comes to us, we are better equipped to face the challenge if we have been trained not to imagine that we have a claim on life, that the world owes us something. When tragedy comes, it is a perfectly normal reaction to cry out in one's pain: "Why did this happen?" There are those who cannot be shaken out of their bitterness, because they regard tragedy as a personal affront to themselves, who had an unlimited account in the bank of life. "How could it happen to *me*?" is their indignant response to the inevitable. Long-drawn-out persistence in mourning is not always a mark of deep devotion to the dead. It often is a banner of war unfurled against life and its Giver; not melancholy, but high dudgeon is the reigning emotion.

The discipline of thanksgiving, which the ritual of prayer seeks to foster, endows men with humility and a sense of balance. When this gift for seeing oneself properly in the scheme of things exists, one finds a deeper capacity for the enjoyment of life in prosperity and a greater measure of strength to bear affliction in adversity. But where the living sense of appreciation for our blessings shrivels up and dies, either through mere disuse or through the vulgar notion that anything in life can be bought and paid for, the moment of triumph finds us arrogant or blasé, and the hour of trial, weak and lacking in staying power.

Robert Gordis
A Faith for Moderns

Thanksgiving Essential to the Religious Life

Standing before the creator God, the Jew recognizes his dependence upon him for life and all its blessings, and acknowledges his duty to render thanks for these. Thanksgiving is thus the basic theme of the classical Jewish liturgy; the most common type of prayer in the siddur is that of adoration, praise, and gratitude. The framers of the liturgy did not regard it as enough to think with David in Browning's "Saul,"

> How good is man's life, the mere living! How fit to employ
> All the heart and the soul and the senses, forever in joy!

One must also turn to the divine source of the gifts and say with Saul's mother,

> Let one more attest,
> I have lived, seen God's hand thro' a lifetime,
> And all was for best.

So fundamental and essential to the religious life did the Talmudic rabbis hold thanksgiving to be that they declared that in the era of Messianic fulfillment all sacrifices would be abolished (since there would no longer be any sins for which to atone) except the sacrifice of thanksgiving, and all prayers would cease except the prayer of thanksgiving (Leviticus Rabbah 9:7). As far as the rabbis were concerned, one ought to thank and praise God for the sorrows as well as the joys of life. What, asks the Talmud, is an "affliction of love?" It answers, one that does not deprive the sufferer of the power to pray (Berachot 5a). As long as prayer is possible, God's chastising hand is felt by the sufferer as laid on him not in anger but in love.

Bernard Martin
Prayer in Judaism

Always Give Thanks

Be not like those who honor their gods in prosperity and curse them in adversity. In pleasure or pain, give thanks!

Rabbi Akiba
Mekilta to Exodus

The Language of Prayer— Appreciation and Yearning

Generally speaking the language of prayer echoes two fundamental states of the soul—the state of appreciation, and that of yearning for the consummation of fulfillment. If the complexities of human emotion be divided into two categories—those resulting from the retreat of the soul and those reflecting its advance into the outer world, then it is the dominance of the latter category that is articulated in worship. Fear, anxiety, selfish ambition, envy, anger, possessiveness and pride—all the attitudes which reflect the recoil of the soul from contact with other beings in the domain of the spirit are expressed in prayer only as springboards from which the soul leaps into the bright sunlight of their corresponding opposites. Thus, a goodly half of prayer consists of hymns, "praising the Lord," whereby our soul articulates its appreciation of the beauty and nobility of existence, echoing the exclamation of God when He beheld His creation, "Behold, it is good." The other half of prayer consists of petitions for the perfection and completion of personality, as if our soul were straining and stretching to grow into the fullness of its ideal being. In both phases of prayer we see the human self rising gradually from the recognition of its own weakness to the perception of the Divine majesty, and thence to the aspiration for the fulfillment of its being. But there is no prayer without the inner assurance that God dwells within us, even as He is in the universe outside our being. And, then, we yearn to expand the walls of our self as far as they would go, so as to allow the utmost room for the growth of His seeds within our soul.

Jacob B. Agus
Guideposts in Modern Judaism

Appreciation and Action

Jewish tradition assigns a special blessing to be recited on seeing a beautiful spectacle of nature. It specifies, moreover, that even a blind person should recite the blessing thanking God for "opening the eyes of the blind" because, though he himself cannot see, nevertheless he benefits from the sight of others. Judaism has never failed to perceive the connection between appreciation and action. He who is aware of his own good fortune is more likely to share it with the less fortunate than he who takes everything as his due. He who perceives the extent to which his welfare is dependent upon his fellowmen will be more apt to serve them in turn than he who is oblivious to their interdependence. And he who regularly reminds himself of the extent to which his whole being is a manifestation of the Creative Power behind and within all things will more probably feel and fulfill his toughest ethical responsibilities. Gratitude for our blessings, then, is more than just a mood worthy on its own account. It also is, or should be, the precursor to that conduct which is the final objective of prayer.

Roland B. Gittelsohn
Man's Best Hope

Thanksgiving Will Not Cease

In the time to come all other sacrifices will cease, but the sacrifice of thanksgiving will not cease. All other prayers will cease, but thanksgiving will not cease.

Leviticus Rabbah 9:7

6 LIVING PRAYER

Life Becomes a Sanctuary

Prayer is aspiration. The self-satisfied disregard it. They who reach for higher things find it a necessity.

Prayer is a discipline. They who seek meaning and purpose in life discover it a wise teacher.

Prayer is an art. We perfect it through practice.

Gradually, the interval between prayer and deed diminishes—until, at last, all life becomes a sanctuary.

Alvin I. Fine
CCAR Journal

Waiting for the Urge

Many of us regretfully refrain from habitual prayer, waiting for an urge that is complete, sudden, and unexampled. But the unexampled is scarce, and perpetual refraining can easily grow into a habit. We may even come to forget what to regret, what to miss.

Abraham Joshua Heschel
Man's Quest for God

Routine Breeds Attention

Why should worship be bound to regular occasions? Why impose a calendar on the soul? Is not regularity of observance a menace to the freedom of the heart?ke

Strict observance of a way of life at fixed times and in identical forms tends to become a matter of routine, of outward compliance. How to prevent observance from becoming stereotyped, mechanical, was, indeed, a perennial worry in the history of Judaism. The cry of the prophet: "Their heart is far from me," was a signal of alarm.

Should I reject the regularity of prayer and rely on the inspiration of the heart and only worship when I am touched by the spirit? Should I resolve: unless the spirit comes, I shall abstain from praying? The deeper truth is that routine breeds attention, calling forth a response where the soul would otherwise remain dormant. One is committed to being affected by the holy, if he abides at the threshold of its realm. Should it be left to every individual to find his own forms of worship whenever the spirit would move him? Yet who is able to extemporize a prayer without falling into the trap of clichés? Moreover, spiritual substance grows in clinging to a source of spirit richer than one's own.

Inspirations are brief, sporadic and rare. In the long interims the mind is often dull, bare and vapid. There is hardly a soul that can radiate more light than it receives. To perform a mitzvah is to meet the spirit. But the spirit is not something we can acquire once and for all but something we must constantly live with and pray for. For this reason the Jewish way of life is to reiterate the ritual, to meet the spirit again and again, the spirit in oneself and the spirit that hovers over all beings.

The spirit rests not only on our achievement, on our goal, but also on our effort, on our way. This is why the very act of going to the house of worship, every day or every seventh day, is a song without words. When done in humility, in simplicity of heart, it is like a child who, eager to hear a song, spreads out the score before its mother. All the child can do is to open the book.

But the song must be forthcoming. We cannot long continue to live on a diet that consists of anticipation plus frustration.

Abraham Joshua Heschel
Man's Quest for God

Prayer Assigned a Place of Primacy in the Life of the Jew

The rabbis assigned to prayer a place of primacy in the life of the Jew. The Jew is required not only to participate in the prescribed daily services in synagogue and at home, but also to pronounce blessings on all events and experiences. As the famous scholar M. Steinschneider aptly put it: "The Jew's whole life became a divine service with interruptions." And these rabbinic prayers have withstood the vicissitudes of time and fashion and have survived the onslaughts of both persecution and prosperity. It is only in our times that these prayers have been challenged. If the challenge is to be met succesfully an understanding of these prayers is urgently needed.

Abraham Millgram
Jewish Worship

Hidden Yearnings

Prayer is at the heart not only of great religion but of significant living.
Without prayer we cannot scale the heights of compassion or attain the peaks of love of our fellow man of which we are capable.
Prayer has been an enduring and universal phenomenon of human life, not because a priesthood ordained it, nor because tradition hallowed it, but because man is ever seeking to probe into his own depths and bring to light his hidden yearnings.

Morris Adler
Shaarey Zedek Recorder

Prayer—Confronting the Divine Presence

One may confront God in prayer because all life is a confrontation between God and man. Living with the awareness of the Presence, man is Godward turned. Every undertaking of such a man has something of the nature of an offering to God; it is a prayer enacted. Thus, when praying, the Jew is asked to consider himself confronting the Divine Presence, he is not required to enter into a specific situation of prayer, but by the specific means of prayer to become acutely aware of the human situation of living in the presence of God. Prayer, in Judaism is not an activity apart from life, but a specific form of the Jewish way of life. In Judaism, living means facing God. One lives in the attitude of prayer and one prays in the attitude of living.

Eliezer Berkovits
Studies in Torah Judaism

To Pray Means to Live in an Inner Universe

We live too much in the external world. We live for the most part in a man-made environment. The holidays of our Jewish calendar revolve around the seasons, and every season brought to our forefathers living in a pastoral and agricultural society, some evidence of the wonder and mystery of life. Wherever they looked they saw the handiwork of God. Wherever we look we see man's accomplishments, the products of his ingenuity. We live in an environment in which man's greatness has been projected outward—great buildings, rapid travel, explorations in outer space, great facility in communication, highways, vehicles. All that we have accomplished looks at us from the outside, and we live and we think in terms of the external.

When a man thinks of getting ahead, he thinks of physical, material, tangible things. Prayer requires the cultivation of the delicate, the tender, the mystic inner capacities of man. To pray means to live in an inner universe of feelings, of responses, of emotional and spiritual experiences. Perhaps our inner life has become a little more hollow as we have projected ourselves so completely into the external world. Perhaps we are afraid that if we concentrate on that inner life we might not find very much there, and so we take refuge in the externalities.

Prayer requires that we withdraw into the inner world, that we stimulate and cultivate inner faculties, and the world is too much with us to allow that solitude, that retirement into oneself, that living with oneself, that prayer requires.

Morris Adler
The Voice Still Speaks

We Need to Take Time to Listen

Our tradition is vitally concerned with the proper use of the power of speech. Three times every day we conclude the Amidah with the prayer: "O God keep my tongue from evil and my lips from deceit." But our Sages remind us too that the power to keep silent should also be used frequently and wisely. We often regret having spoken; rarely, having kept silent. In silence there is the opportunity to reflect quietly, to resolve nobly, to probe deeply. In a noisy world, we need to make time to listen to those voices within us and above us which will only be heard when all is hushed around us. Daily the prayer book reminds us too, that we can worship God not only with "the words of my mouth" but also with "the meditations of my heart."

"I need not shout my faith. Thrice eloquent
Are quiet trees and the green listening sod;
Hushed are the stars, whose power is never spent;
The hills are mute. Yet how they speak of God!"

Sidney Greenberg
Temple Sinai News

The prayer of him who has no faith will not be heard.

Nachman of Bratzlav
Likutay Etzot Ha-Shem

Prayer Purifies

Gold and silver become purified through fire. If you feel no sense of improvement after your prayer, you are either made of base metal, or your prayer was cold.

The Koretzer Rabbi
The Hasidic Anthology

God Knows What Is in the Heart

It is written (Isaiah 65:24), "Before they call I will answer. . . . " Rabbi Elazar ben Padat said, If a human being hears the words of a person, he can judge him, but if he does not, he cannot judge him correctly. But God is not like that, for before a person speaks, God knows what is in his heart.

Exodus Rabbah 21:3

Some Can, and Some Cannot

The problem of prayer is inextricably bound up with our view of man. If man is really a self-sufficient creature, if he is in no need of support from a Reality beyond himself, and if he is so self-sufficient that he does not even look upon himself as a "creature," then, indeed, man—ancient or modern—cannot pray. If, on the other hand, man relies on spiritual strength and support coming from outside of himself, if, that is to say, he knows himself to be a creature, though he may also know himself to be needed by God as a junior partner in the ongoing work of creation, then modern man can pray. . . .

"Modern man," as pre-modern man before him, must, from time to time, check the contents of his prayers against the nature of his "God concept." The reach of prayer may, and should, outdistance the grasp of our philosophical and theological definitions. God, to be God, must be greater than our concepts of Him. But true prayer cannot very well voice strivings and aspirations which run counter to the very nature of God as we conceive of Him. This seems to be the profound truth behind the Rabbinic requirement that the creedal element of the Jewish worship service (i.e., the Shema and its Blessings) *precede* the prayer of petition.

We have been trying to provide some perspective and background for the question, "Can Modern Man Pray?" We have seen that some of the problems which trouble us are problems which have equally troubled our predecessors. We have also noted that one's ability to pray depends, in the final analysis, upon his ability to see himself as as creature of God. There are those who have this ability, and there are those who do not. But this "creature feeling" is something far too personal to be amenable to debate. That is why we have to end our answer as we have begun it. Can modern man pray? Some can, and some cannot.

Jakob J. Petuchowski
1967 CCAR Proceedings

"Ye shall serve the Lord . . . and He will bless thy bread" (Exodus 23:25). One eats by oneself, even in company, but should pray in communion with all Israel, even when alone.

Mendel of Kotzk
quoted by Martin Buber in
Tales of the Hasidim

Understand What Is in My Heart

It is written, "Listen to my words, O God, understand my meditation . . ."(Psalm 5:2). King David said, "Master of the universe: When I have the strength to stand before You in prayer and express my words, listen to me. But when I do not have the strength, understand what is in my heart."

Midrash Tehillim 5:6

Prayer Involves Self Improvement

The prophet Isaiah, 8th century B.C.E., taught that a prayer prompted by greed and not motivated by ethical striving would not be answered. He proclaimed in the name of God,

"When you spread your hands to pray,
I will hide mine eyes from you . . .
Yea, when you make many prayers,
I will not hear
. . . Wash you, make you clean,
Put away the evil of your doings
. . . Seek justice, relieve the oppressed . . ."

Isaiah 1:15–17

Isaiah taught that the person who performed deeds of justice and compassion would find God waiting to communicate with him. A word which the Hebrews have used for prayer is *"t'filah,"* which comes from the verb which has been translated *"to judge oneself."* Prayer involves self-judgment, self-improvement. It is a step towards the service of that which is holy and just, a path to the loving-giving life. Isaiah further teaches that if you have helped your neighbor in distress, if you have fed the hungry, clothed the naked, and aided those who are persecuted wrongly, if *then* you call, the Lord will answer you. If you cry for aid, He will say, *"Here I am!"* (Isaiah 58:6–9). It is but a summary of this teaching to say, when the man who strives for righteousness prays, he will be strengthened in his being and in his work. Are these not the legitimate goals of prayer?

Herbert M. Baumgard
Judaism and Prayer

The Divine Unity Becomes Man's Task

"Teach me Thy way, O Lord; I will walk in Thy truth; unite my heart to fear Thy name" (Psalm 86:11). This sentence of the Psalms has acquired an even richer meaning in Jewish thought, not only for its mysticism and philosophy, but also as an expression of the people's meditation and prayer. For the sentence tells of the one heart which finds its way to the One God and the one command. If man attains this one heart and consequently follows the one path, then he has gained true reverence for the One God: he thereby brings monotheism to its genuine realization. As the ancient Hebrew morning prayer says, man "unifies God" through his love for him. In this desire to "unify God," man's creative impulse finds a powerful means of self-expression. Through his moral action man creates the unity of God upon earth, and thus even the divine unity becomes, as it were, man's task.

Leo Baeck
The Essence of Judaism

Rabbi Elazar said: Prayer is greater than good deeds. No one had more good deeds than Moses, but still he was only answered when he prayed.

Berachot 32b

Twin Paths

Religion has always insisted that the highway of God is open to every man. He is free to walk the twin paths of worship and of action. Action expresses itself through ritual and through the ethical life; worship, pre-eminently through prayer.

Robert Gordis
The Ladder of Prayer

A Word Uttered in Prayer Is a Promise

Prayer must not be dissonant with the rest of living. The mercifulness, gentleness, which pervades us in moments of prayer is but a ruse or a bluff, if it is inconsistent with the way we live at other moments. The divorce of liturgy and living, of prayer and practice, is more than a scandal; it is a disaster. A word uttered in prayer is a promise, an earnest, a commitment. If the promise is not kept, we are guilty of violating a promise.

Abraham Joshua Heschel
Judaism

As We Speak to God, He Speaks to Us

Humility is the consciousness of our place in the world; but it is a place not merely given to us but created by us. Without knowledge of the moral commandment there can therefore be no true humility or faith. Only the two united result in self-knowledge and permit us to experience life in totality; they constitute the religious feeling toward life which unites what is given to us and what we in turn have to give. As man speaks to his God he always hears God's words; during his prayer he always simultaneously hears the commandments to duty. This simultaneity, also characteristic of monotheism, gives to man his inner unity and religiousness.

That is why the Bible places faith and deed together, as a single religious unit. "Keep love and justice, and wait on thy God continually" (Hosea 12:7). "Trust in the Lord, and do good" (Psalm 37:3). "Wait on the Lord, and keep his way" (Psalm 37:34). "Offer the sacrifices of righteousness, and put your trust in the Lord" (Psalm 4:6). "Seek ye the Lord, all ye meek of the earth, who have wrought his justice; seek righteousness, seek meekness" (Zephaniah 2:3). "He hath shewed thee, O man, what is good; and what doth the Lord require of thee, but to do justly, and to love mercy, and to walk humbly with thy God" (Micah 6:8). In this last sentence, humility is seen as the spiritual result of righteousness and love put into practice; but at the same time, humility is a beginning, for it is a humility which never rests but always seeks afresh to apply God's word. Arising from the ethical deed it also gives rise to a new ethical deed.

Leo Baeck
The Essence of Judaism

To Live Out the Dreams of Prayer

Prayer takes us from the noise of the world into the stillness of the soul, not so that we may escape from the world into some mountain retreat or island monastery, but to return us into the world there to perform our task. Before he could know how to lead his people out of Egypt, Moses had to experience the shepherd's solitude in the land of Midian where God found him at the burning bush. The Baal Shem spent the early years of his life in a mountain retreat and far from society. There he strengthened the bonds which joined him to the divine, until he was prepared to disclose his identity and engage in his holy work of redemption. So it is with all of us. Prayer removes us from the marketplace and the counting-chamber to heal us, to wash us clean, to purify us, to strengthen us, to remind us of what we have forgotten, to let our souls touch the Source of all souls, and then to send us back to the crossroads of life so that we may live out the dreams of prayer.

Samuel H. Dresner
Prayer, Humility, and Compassion

To Petition Him Means to Pledge Ourselves

"True worship," wrote Emil Hirsch, "is not a petition to God. It is a sermon to ourselves." And that is why, for example, the Shema is followed immediately by a host of orders addressed to us. "Thou shalt love the Lord thy God. Thou shalt teach these words diligently to thy children. Thou shalt speak of them. Thou shalt bind them. Thou shalt write them." This prayer is concerned with our behavior most explicitly.

But even when the prayer is not directly addressed to us, even when the prayer is addressed to God, there is implied in it the understanding that we and God work together for the realization and the fulfillment of those prayers. In the Jewish view of things you and I are engaged in a great partnership, in a partnership with God. And we are expected to be active partners. We are expected to work for those things in which we believe and which we would like to see come to pass.

I hope this won't sound blasphemous or irreverent but I think that a mature understanding of God must include an awareness of God's helplessness. As children, we are taught to believe that God is omnipotent. He can do everything. Well, He can't, as a matter of fact.

There is not a single affliction from which we suffer—war, poverty, pollution, injustice, racial strife—that God can remove without our cooperation. There is not a single blessing we crave—world peace, food and shelter for all, clean air, a just society, domestic tranquility—that God can bring without our cooperation. A mature understanding of God looks upon Him neither as a miracle worker, nor a magician, nor as a Messiah who provides instant cure for all the world's ills. God is the power who works in us and through us to enable us to achieve those things that our faith in Him assures us are capable of coming into being.

Without us the most important tasks in the world will remain undone. That is why our requests of God imply commitment of ourselves. To petition Him means to pledge ourselves. Our prayers become meaningful when we do everything we can to make them come true. "Prayer," wrote Santayana, "is not a substitute for work; it is a desperate effort to work further and to be efficient beyond the range of one's powers." Our prayers are answered when they enable us to act as God desires.

Sidney Greenberg
Hidden Hungers

When You Share

When you share your bread with the hungry,
Bring the outcast poor to your house,
When you see the naked and clothe them,
Hide yourself not from your own flesh. . . .
Then you shall call, and God shall answer,
You shall cry out, and He will say, "I am here."

Isaiah 58:7,9

By benevolence a man rises to a height where he meets God. Therefore do a good deed before you begin your prayers.

Ahai Gaon
Sheiltot

I Was Hungry

I was hungry
and you formed a humanities club
and discussed my hunger. Thank you.
I was imprisoned
and you crept off quietly
to your chapel in the cellar
and prayed for my release.
I was naked and in your mind
you debated the morality of my
appearance.
I was sick
and you knelt and thanked God for
your health.
I was homeless
and you preached to me

of the spiritual shelter of God.

I was lonely
and you left me alone
to pray for me.
You seem so holy;
so close to God
But I'm still very hungry
and lonely
and cold.
So where have your prayers gone?
What have they done?
What does it profit a man
to page through his book of prayers
when the rest of the world
is crying for his help?

Author Unknown

Rabbi Eleazar would give a coin to the poor, and would then worship. He said: It is written, "I will greet You with charity" (Psalm 17:15).

Bava Batra 10a

The Most Important Outcome of Prayer Is Action

Judaism does not agree with those who cherish prayer as an end in itself and would therefore value a life devoted entirely to contemplation and prayer. It looks upon prayer rather as a means to the more important end of a nobler spiritual and ethical life. Thus the Talmud records a conversation in which the Roman Emperor Antoninus asked Rabbi Judah why it would not be proper to praise God every hour of the day. The rabbi replied: "In order not to mock God, this is forbidden." Antoninus expressed dissatisfaction. Rabbi Judah approached him early the next morning and said to him: "Hail, O lord!" An hour later he came to him again and said: "Peace, O king!" Another hour later he appeared yet again before the emperor, with: "Rule forever, O mighty one!" At this point Antoninus protested: "Why do you mock at majesty?" To which Judah responded: "Let your ears hear what your mouth speaks! If you, a king of flesh and blood, say this when greeted hourly, what shall be said of one who mocks the King of kings, the Holy One?"

All of which adds up to the inescapable conclusion that by far the most important outcome of prayer is action. Without ensuing action, even the most eloquent prayer is like a stage set for a symphony concert—instruments tuned and in place, music opened to the proper score, audience pleasantly expectant—but the musicians' chairs occupied by men who cannot play. The English word *pray* comes from a Latin root meaning *to beg or to entreat*. The Hebrew word *pray* comes from a root meaning *to judge oneself*. The difference is crucial. The former is an outworn notion of prayer, incongruous with our present-day knowledge and experience. The latter is a mature concept, consistent in every way with what we know, conducive to conduct through which we glorify God by fulfilling ourselves.

There is a special impetus which sincere prayer can give to improved ethical behavior. It arises from the fact that in prayer there is no need to save face. So often, when we are chastised or even gently reproached by others, we find ourselves bristling with resistance, straining to defend ourselves against what we construe as attack. When we pray, no one is attacking; hence there is no need for defense. No one is even listening as we evaluate our own conduct. If ever a man can afford to be impeccably honest with himself—without need to rationalize or prettify—it is in prayer. This is therefore one of his most promising ways to understand himself with keener insight, to acknowledge his deficiencies in truth and to take his first hesitant steps toward self-improvement.

Roland B. Gittelsohn
Man's Best Hope

The Sanctification of God's Name

The summit of moral action is the performance of deeds that hallow God's name, and conversely the most reprehensive of immoral action is the desecration of God's name. This principle is stated forcefully in the Bible:

"You shall not profane My holy name, that I may be sanctified in the midst of the Israelite people" (Leviticus 22:32). To be sure, Israel sanctifies God's name when the congregation recites the Kaddish and exclaims: "Magnified and sanctified be His great name," and when the congregation recites the Kedushah: "We will sanctify Thy name in the world even as they sanctify it in the highest heaven." But it is more important to hallow God's name by moral action, so that men shall see and say that the God of Israel is the true God. Extraordinary acts of justice and compassion, when performed in the sight of the Gentiles, are kiddush hashem, the sanctification of God's name. Acts that reflect dishonor on the Jewish faith, such as defrauding a Gentile, are hillul hashem, the desecration of God's name, for people judge Judaism by the conduct of Jews.

The spiritual hero in Judaism is the martyr who hallows God's name with his very soul. The precedent for kiddush hashem through martyrdom was set by Rabbi Akiba, a second century teacher. The Talmud relates that Rabbi Akiba defied the Roman decree forbidding the Jews to study and practice the teachings of the Torah. He was apprehended, tortured, and executed for his defiance of the Roman edict. The time of his execution happened to be "the hour for the recital of the Shema." While the Romans were torturing him and "combing his flesh with iron combs," Akiba recited the Shema. His disciples, seeing this, marveled and asked: "Our teacher, even to this point?" Akiba answered:

"All my days I have been troubled by this verse,

> 'Thou shalt love the lord thy God with all thy heart, with all thy soul, and with all thy might,' which I interpret 'even if He takes thy soul.' . . . When shall I have the opportunity of fulfilling this? Now that I have the opportunity shall I not fulfill it?" He prolonged the word *ehad* (one) until he expired while saying it (Berachot 61b).

Rabbi Akiba's example has been emulated by numerous Jews, and martyrdom has come to be regarded in Judaism as the highest religious triumph. Since the martyr's act of self-sacrifice is performed before the very eyes of his persecutors, his deed bears weighty witness to Israel's loyalty to God. By his defiance of evil and suffering, the martyr confirms the Jew's spiritual potential. The martyr, as it were, crowns God as the Holy One of Israel.

One of the great scholars, Rabbi Asher (1250-1327), composed an ethical work entitled *Rules*. In it he offers advice on how to pray, and especially how to recite the Shema:

> Pray not as a matter of rote, for prayer is the service of the heart. . . . And when thou recitest the verse which bids thee love the Lord thy God, speak as one ready to deliver up life and substance for the sanctification of God, thus fulfilling the words of the Psalmist: "For Thy sake are we killed all the day" (Psalm 44:23).

In the Middle Ages the Church performed many an auto-da-fé to burn heretics *ad majorem dei gloriam*, and many a Jew offered his soul, not for God's glory but for God's holiness. The opportunities to sanctify God's name were frequent. Many a Jew, faced with the choice between apostasy and a martyr's death, chose to die for kiddush hashem.

Abraham Millgram
Jewish Worship

One May Confront God in the Mitzvah

In which sense do we call prayer a specific form of Jewish living? Is it a more intense form of confrontation, does it establish a more intimate relationship between man and God? Within the framework of Judaism, it is difficult to agree to the suggestion. One may *pray* with little awareness of the Presence, just as some unusual religious personalities have *lived* in ever-renewed intimacy with it. Theoretically, it is possible for one to be a pious Jew in the strictest orthodox sense of the word without ever uttering a word of prayer. Those of whom it may be said that *Toratan Umnatam*, that the study of the Torah is their sole life occupation, do not have to pray. This is not so because one can live as a Jew without prayer, but because whatever one does fulfilling oneself as a Jew is not essentially different from praying. For many generations, numberless Jews studying the pages of the Talmud have experienced the nearness of God, and have had a sense of intimacy with Him, not surpassed in intensity by the prayer of the most devout. Sitting at the Sabbath meal, as a part of the sanctification of the day of rest, Jews may have a realization of living under the providential eyes of God no less intense than any which might be accomplished by the means of prayer. A Jew preoccupied with the performance of a Mitzvah does not need to interrupt his activity for the sake of prayer. Any deed performed in the name of God is not essentially different from prayer. In the Mitzvah one may confront God no less than in prayer.

Eliezer Berkovits
Studies in Torah Judaism

In Prayer We Find Strength

In prayer we find strength for life. Temptation and passion, as well as irritation and torment, plague us constantly. Each day has its ordeals, and at times we wonder if we shall survive them. There comes a time in the life of each of us when everything crumbles at our feet; all the supports upon which we were accustomed to lean—wealth, possessions, friends, relatives—slip away into nothingness. When death takes a loved one, a yawning void opens in our lives that nothing seems to fill; the petty thoughts we have, the small talk we indulge in, the day to day routine of our habits—sleeping and eating, working and playing—suddenly appear cheap and unworthy. When failure is our lot and that upon which we had set our hearts, for which we had labored long and hoped for fervently, is lost to us—a love unrequited, a child turned wayward, a friend untrue, a promise broken—despair settles upon us. When without warning calamity comes—a business disaster, a painful illness, a consuming disease, a broken limb, a broken heart—the dark mantle of melancholy casts its pall over us and we are enveloped by a cloud of meaninglessness and bitterness and foreboding which threatens to take the taste of the joy of living from our mouths. Our days are filled with gloom and we begin to sink beyond the helpful words of friends and the bright light of the sun into the dark misery of our own heart, alone and forsaken, broken and defeated.

At times of death and failure and despair, when we can turn to no one else—for no one else understands, no one else seems to care, no one else will really listen—we turn to God. Prayer breaks forth. And comfort comes.

Samuel H. Dresner
Prayer, Humility, and Compassion

Our prayers are answered not when we are given what we ask but when we are challenged to be what we can be.

Morris Adler
National Jewish Monthly

The Most Authentic Testimony of Prayer

How can I pray with another human being if I do not know the *needs* of that other? What does it mean to pray together if I do not have the *consent* of the others with whom I pray? But the others may say to me in the course of this process, "Care about me first as a person! Cease oppressing me or merely 'using' me as a member of your religious community. Help me be free enough to join in this search in *my own* way." When we realize that ultimately we are necessarily joined in a prayer community to all of humanity, since the light of each and every soul is needed for the ultimate *tikkun ha-shekhinah*, the restoration of the One great light, there is no escaping the real life demands that being a person of prayer makes upon us. Here prayer and action are completely united with one another, and for many action itself will speak as the loudest and most authentic testimony of prayer.

Arthur Green
The Reconstructionist

Constancy Sanctifies

It is not by the rare act of greatness that character is determined, but by everyday actions, by a constant effort to rend our callousness. It is constancy that sanctifies. Judaism is an attempt to place all of life under the glory of ultimate significance, to relate all scattered actions to the One. Through the constant rhythm of prayers, disciplines, reminders, joys, man is taught not to forfeit his grandeur.

Abraham Joshua Heschel
God in Search of Man

A Resource for Living

When men succeed in mastering the full art of prayer, they will have gained an inestimable resource for living with courage, insight, and joy. In the dark hours of trial and suffering which are inescapable in the human situation, prayer helps men to face life without fear or bitterness, knowing that the light will dawn, whether from within or from without. In the days of well-being and prosperity, when men's eyes tend to be blinded by the sunshine, the practice of prayer gives them insight into reality, the capacity to see the Maker behind the made, the Master in His creation. With the deepened sense of thanksgiving one's joy in life grows, as one experiences each day the miracle of creation. In essence, all man's prayers are an echo of the voice of the youthful Jacob at Beth-el: "Indeed, God is in this place, and I did not know it."

Robert Gordis
A Faith for Moderns

A Most Reliable Source of Energy

We are a generation in search for ever new sources of energy. We have raised coal and oil from the earth, harnessed rivers, transformed the rays of the sun and split the atom. But in our restless search for energy, we have abandoned one of man's most ancient and reliable sources of energy, namely, prayer. What power reserve is available to us at those low moments which we experience almost daily in the cyclical rhythm of our emotional lives? The genuinely religious personalities of all generations systematically derived the power to overcome these frequent and inevitable power shortages from daily prayer.

Source Unknown

The answer to our prayer may be the echo of our resolve.

Herbert Louis Samuel
Belief and Action

God Says "Hineni"

If God does not reply, what kind of response can we expect? The response which God gave to the suffering and questing Job, "I am God." Whatever exists responds to us. The flower responds to my touch. The violin responds to the box. The tide responds to the tug of the moon. At Gloucester in Massachusetts, I climbed down the ancient boulders, witnesses of the Ice Age, and sat alone as the tide began to pound against the rocks, slowly engulfing them. That tide came in at the exact moment which had been ordained for it at that place. It was responding. And God responds to man. How? By disclosing Himself to us. God hears prayer, not by fulfilling our requirements, not by satisfying our needs, but by making Himself known to us as a living reality in our lives. When we pray we become aware, like Moses who sought to know who God was, that God "is what He is." But even more important than I should hear is that I should address myself to God. Not that He needs it, but that I need it. I need to feed and nurture my soul. I need to feel awe. I need to be aware of my finiteness and the wonder of my existence. I need to be reminded of this daily. Most important, I need to affirm, to say "Yes," to say "I do." I cannot exist if I assume the destructive attitude of one of Sartre's characters: "I have decided that all along death has been the secret of my life, that I have lived for the purpose of dying. I die in order to demonstrate the impossibility of living; my eyes will put an extinguisher upon the earth and shut it down forever."

When I call, it can be that God will make Himself manifest. Not always. Even a psalmist in an age of faith cried out, "Do not hide your presence from me." But another psalmist wrote, "I called and God responded." Men in the Bible have responded to God's call, "Hineni, here I am." God, too, says, "Hineni." For some, this is not enough. For others, it is.

David Polish
The Theological Foundations of Prayer

Every Word Makes an Impression

Many days and years may pass, and it may seem that you are accomplishing nothing with your prayers. Do not give up, for every word makes an impression. It is written, "Water wears away stone" (Job 14:19). It may seem that water dripping on a stone will not a make any impression, but after many years, it can actually make a hole in the stone. This can actually be demonstrated. Your heart may be like a stone. It may seem that your words of prayer make no impression on it whatsoever. Still, as the days and years pass, even your heart of stone will be penetrated.

Nachman of Bratzlav
Likutay Etzot Ha-Shem

The Difference that Prayer Makes

The difference between one who prays and one who does not pray is not to be found in the fact that the former sets aside time every day for his prayer, while the latter does not. There is a more basic dichotomy. The types of lives those two people live are thoroughly different. The time devoted to prayer makes an impression upon every aspect of the entire day.

Abraham Isaac Kook
Olat Re'iyah

Conversing with God

Converse with God, and consider carefully what is your purpose in life. Delve into yourself, and beg God to help you find Him. Use whatever language you speak best, and argue with God, petitioning Him in every way. . . .

If you set aside a time each day to converse with God, you will be worthy of finding Him. You may do this for days and years with no apparent effect, but in the end you will reach your goal.

Nachman of Bratzlav
Sefer Ha-Middot

The Efficacy of Prayer

What according to the Tradition is the efficacy of prayer? Does it avail?

That God responds to prayer is a basic belief of Judaism.

On the extent of the response the Jewish faithful disagree, some being optimists or maximalists on the issue; others, if not pessimists, are at least circumspect or minimalist.

All Jews acknowledge the conditions and limits of prayer we have listed. Even the most sanguine concede further that it does not replace human effort. One should not address God, fold his hands, and wait for his wish to come true—at least not if one is true to Judaism. One prays but works, too. A sick man calls on God but on his physician also. Otherwise, the Tradition holds, he is a sinner against his own soul and against God who endowed the surgeon with his skill and the drugs with their properties.

Given the right use, prayer may, in the Jewish view, achieve the following:

It can first of all—and on this all religious Jews are agreed—release pent-up feelings, crystallize inarticulate thoughts, muster the will, and all in all prove of great psychological worth.

It can further—and on this too there is general assent—tap levels of personality otherwise not to be reached, setting free the full resources of the spirit.

On why prayer possesses this peculiar potency the circumspect and the optimists differ. The former contend that the process is purely naturalistic, being the very normal response of man's psyche to an idea as compelling as that of God. The latter are far bolder, holding that in prayer man is inundated by the divine; an experience quite beyond natural law and not to be accounted for by it.

All religious Jews agree next that prayer exerts an influence on things outside man. But once again there is disagreement on the *how*. The minimalists maintain that prayer sways the physical world only through human agencies. The maximalists insist that quite apart from man it impinges directly on reality.

Then, is the maximalist position that the sky, as it were, is the limit, that prayer can accomplish any result whatsoever?

On this point the maximalists themselves divide. Some argue that prayer must function within natural law as science describes it and that no accomplishment is to be awaited beyond its confines.

Others, super-maximalists as they may be called, contend that nature is but a tool in God's hand. Nothing then can be impossible, not even a miracle. For, as Scripture asks: "Can anything be too wonderful for God?"

Religious Jews, it should be clear by now, run a wide gamut in their evaluation of prayer.

Milton Steinberg
Basic Judaism

7 THE SIDDUR— A TREASURE HOUSE

What Is Special about Jewish Prayer

Jewish prayer is prayer that uses the idiom of the Hebrew Bible and reflects the Jewish soul. It is prayer that expresses the basic values of the Jewish people and affirms the central articles of Jewish faith. It is prayer that reflects our historical experience and gives expression to our future aspirations. When the prayer of a Jewish person does not reflect one of these components, he may be praying, but it cannot be said that he is praying as a Jew.

A Jew may choose his own words when praying to God; but when he uses the words of the siddur, he becomes part of a people. He identifies with Jews everywhere who use the same words and express the same thoughts. He affirms the principle of mutual responsibility and concern. He takes his place at the dawn of history as he binds himself to Abraham, Isaac, and Jacob. He asserts his rights to a Jewish future in this world and to personal redemption in the World-to-Come.

Hayim Halevi Donin
To Pray as a Jew

An Intelligent Piety

All liturgies are rooted in the nature of man and his relationship to the universe in which he lives. One can trace a number of these common roots to ancient man's fears of the inhospitable world that he inhabited. In periods of danger or distress he instinctively turned to the gods for protection and succor. And in time of deliverance and exaltation he naturally praised and thanked the gods for their benevolence. In time liturgies were developed and rituals took shape. To be sure, the concepts of the deities differed from people to people. But they were adequate within their specific cultures.

There were, from time to time, some sensitive souls who were not fully satisfied with the existing liturgies and rituals. They searched for the significance of life and the role of the gods in the affairs of man. This spiritual search often led them, as it still does, to an intellectual impasse. These exceptional men were often troubled by the mysteries of life and death, and not infrequently they experienced the anguish of loneliness. Out of these spiritual struggles came many of the noblest prayers both in Judaism and in other faiths. But less gifted men, who constitute the overwhelming majority of mankind, when faced with similar perplexities of the spirit cannot find the appropriate words to express the yearnings of their hearts. They naturally turn to priests and prophets for the formulation of their prayers.

The liturgy of the synagogue, though sharing many of its characteristics with the liturgies of other faiths, is nonetheless unique. This uniqueness can be grasped partly through a knowledge of its incomparable history. Although the Jewish liturgy had its beginnings in the sacrificial cult of the Jerusalem Temple, it developed into a revolutionary form: public prayer, now shared by many other faiths. It was Judaism that eliminated the sacrificial cult and the priest as an intermediary between the worshiper and the Deity. The Jews were the pioneers in the daring concept that the people can collectively pray directly to God. Since people cannot compose original prayers, the Jews utilized the prayers composed by the gifted—the psalmists and the sages. These prayers remained oral for over a millennium, during which they slowly took shape. In order that these prayers might emanate from their heart, the rabbis insisted on devotion and concentration during worship. This combination of an established liturgy and an earnestness of heart saved the Jewish prayers from becoming mere incantations and resulted, as George Foot Moore put it, in "an intelligent piety."

Abraham Millgram
Jewish Worship

A Bridge across the Ages

The standard prayers, the oldest nucleus of the liturgy, always and everywhere became the center of Jewish worship, a bond of union despite geographical dispersal and a bridge across the ages linking the present with the past. At the same time, each period and place was left free, if not encouraged, to speak its own mind in new compositions added to or inserted within the ancient prayers. . . . Within the larger brotherhood of Israel and the stock of prayers common to all generations, the medieval synagogue attempts and maintains both a contemporary note and regional differences.

Shalom Spiegel
The Jews, Their History, Culture and Religion

The Most Important Single Jewish Book

I regard our old Jewish siddur as the most important single Jewish book, a more personal expression, a closer record of Jewish sufferings, Jewish needs, Jewish hopes and aspirations, than the Bible itself: which for one thing is too grand and universal to be exclusively Jewish (as Shakespeare is not the typical Englishman), and for another, whatever is quintessentially needed for daily use has been squeezed out of it into the prayerbook and so made our daily own. And if you want to know what Judaism is—the question which has no answer if debated on the plane of intellectual argument—you can find out by absorbing that book. The Jewish soul is mirrored there as nowhere else, mirrored or rather embodied there: the *individual's* soul in his private sorrows, and the *people's* soul in its historic burdens, its heroic passion and suffering, its unfaltering faith, through the ages.

Henry Slonimsky
Gates of Understanding

We Are Released from a Sense of Isolation

Jews have long considered that God speaks to man through the events of history. The Decalogue begins with an assertion that is no commandment at all: "I am the Lord thy God, who brought thee out of the land of Egypt, out of the house of bondage" (Exodus 20:2).

The reminder of the Exodus from Egypt permeates every Jewish holiday and religious service. This was, for us, a dramatic period of God-discovery, and it has helped to sustain us for thousands of years, in spite of suffering and wandering. The Exodus has eternally etched on the Jewish soul the conviction that "There is One who helps to save. There is a Power that makes for freedom." The burning memory of our historically recorded relationship with God has helped to keep us alive. This memory is not a detached one. It is a recall of personal experience. It happened to us! We experienced the power of God!

Our Bible states that every Jew, including those yet to be born, stood at Sinai. All Jews are bidden to make the revelation at Sinai a personal experience. Our prayer service today is deliberately conceived to prepare the worshiper to enter into and to make personal to himself the experience of his fathers. This is why so much of our prayer seems to be an historic lesson, a method of teaching, rather than of petition. This is a unique feature of Hebraic prayer. It joins the individual to the community of past, present, and future, and insists that this is one ongoing community.

So much of our Synagogue prayer is in this spirit. Those who participate in our services in an understanding way are released from their sense of isolation and loneliness, and they are linked to the continuing history of an ancient people whose ultimate goals are uplifting to the spirit. In Jewish prayer, the limited strength of the individual is bound to the strength of an enduring Israel and to the eternal God to whom Israel has always related.

Herbert M. Baumgard
Judaism and Prayer

The Prayer Book—Israel's Personal Diary

More than a mere manual of devotion the prayer book is in a sense—Israel's personal diary, catching, as in a series of exquisite vignettes, the scenes and moments of her life, and recording, in a diversity of moods and styles, her deepest and most intimate emotions. Here, for those who have eyes and ears, is Sinai on the one hand, and Belsen on the other; the gleaming courts of the Temple, and the peeling walls of a Polish *klaus*; the blare of the silver trumpets, and the singsong of the Talmud student; the colonnaded walks of a Spanish town, and the narrow, winding lanes of

Safed. Here is a Gabirol effortlessly bringing down the immortal to earth, and a Rhineland cantor scribbling his earthiness into immortality. Here is Luria panting desperately after the Celestial Chariot, and Kallir pinning the glories of God to an acrostic.

T. H. Gaster
Commentary

The Siddur Evokes National Memories and Hopes

The prayers and benedictions, the psalms and hymns, the joyous thanksgivings and mournful dirges which constitute the component parts of the siddur evoke not only emotions, but also national memories and hopes. The prayers of the siddur are the precipitates of the profoundest Jewish historic experiences. Through its contents one can glimpse the panorama of Jewish history from the earliest time to our own day. The redemption from Egyptian slavery, the victory of the Hasmoneans over their Syrian oppressors, the destruction of the Temple by the Romans, the massacres of whole Jewish communities by the Crusaders, the modern struggle for a national home in the land of Israel are but a few of the historic events that are celebrated or lamented in the prayers of the synagogue. But the siddur can bring one into contact with the broad sweep of Jewish history only if he knows the story of the Jewish people, at least the peak events that gave rise to the national outbursts of joyful thanksgiving or sorrowful mourning.

Abraham Millgram
Jewish Worship

Man's Prayer as a Social Being

Man is not himself only, he is a participant in his community. Hence it is not enough that he shall address God in his solitariness; he must turn to Him in his other aspect as well.

Man's prayer as a social being is worship.

Worship does not have to be public, though that is its most usual circumstance; nor need it follow a pre-established program as to text and rite, though it almost always does. Any prayer or ceremonial is worship if it voices either the community or a single person speaking as a member of the group.

The Tradition expects the Jew to set up his private relationship with God, to confront Him when and as the spirit moves him.

"Would that a man might pray the livelong day," was the hope of an ancient rabbi.

But a Jew is also an Israelite, a fellow in the Jewish people. Wherefore Judaism has established a schedule of times and seasons at which he shall come to God in this capacity. It has laid down the principles he shall affirm on such occasions, the ideals he shall assert, even the *personal* expectations which, being a Jew, he ought to entertain. It has gone so far as to work out the very words and ritual gestures in which all these are to be expressed. For this is the nature of the accepted Jewish prayerbooks for weekdays, Sabbaths, festivals, and holy days: they state the fundamental minimal aspirations required of a traditional Jew on his own behalf and cherished by Jewry as a collectivity.

Milton Steinberg
Basic Judaism

The Prayer Book Was Never Completed

In a time sequence the prayer book may be looked upon as a link between Bible and Talmud, each link in the chain overlapping the preceding one. Thus, the prayer book arose before the later books of the Bible were completed and the early days of talmudic development exercised a considerable influence on the prayer book which had achieved its classic form while the Talmud was still in its earlier stages.

The literary and spiritual tradition which these three books represent never completely came to an end. Long after the Bible canon was closed and no more books admitted into Sacred Scripture, biblical study continued and has become a permanent part of world literature. Long after the Talmud was finished (about the year five hundred), talmudic studies continued through the ages. But even with regard to this continuance of creative work, the prayer book differs from the other two books. While the Bible itself was finally completed about the middle of the second century of the present era and the Talmud in the sixth century, the prayer book itself was never actually completed. All through the centuries new prayers in prose and poetry were added to it. In the periods when mystic moods dominated Jewish life, mystic and cabalistic prayers were added to the prayer book. In periods when philosophic studies flourished, philosophic ideas were inserted, and during times of persecution and exile, poems of tragedy were added.

These various additions were used by the congregations as authentic parts of the prayer book. Indeed, when the Reform movement began no one dreamed of making additions or changes in the Bible or the Talmud. These books were finished and complete for all time. But it was natural to make changes, additions, and subtractions in the prayer book since it was expected to fit the mood and the ideas of the people. Thus, of the three works which Judaism brought out of antiquity, the prayer book was the only one which constantly changed to fit the needs and the moods and the aspirations of the people of Israel.

Solomon B. Freehof
The Small Sanctuary

A Liturgy in Which Gems of Spiritual Fervour Glitter

They prayed metaphysics, acrostics, angelology, Cabbalah, history, exegetics, Talmudical controversies, menus, recipes, priestly prescriptions, the canonical books, psalms, love-poems, an undigested hotch-potch of exalted and questionable sentiments, of communal and egoistic aspirations of the highest order. It was a wonderful liturgy, as grotesque as it was beautiful; like an old cathedral, in all styles of architecture, stored with shabby antiquities and sideshows, and overgrown with moss and lichen, a heterogeneous blend of historical strata of all periods, in which gems of poetry and pathos and spiritual fervour glittered, and pitiful records of ancient persecutions lay petrified. And the method of praying these things was equally complex and uncouth, equally the bondslave of tradition; here a rising and there a bow, now three steps backwards and now a beating of the breast, this bit for the congregation and that for the minister; variants of a page, a word, a syllable, even a vowel, ready for every possible contingency. Their religious consciousness was largely a musical box: the thrill of the ram's horn, the cadenza of a psalmic phrase, the jubilance of a festival "Amen" and the sobriety of a workaday "Amen," the Passover melodies, and the Pentecost, the minor keys of Atonement and the hilarious rhapsodies of Rejoicing, the plainchant of the Law and the more ornate intonation of the Prophets—all this was known and loved, and was far more important than the meaning of it all, or its relation to their real lives: for page upon page was gabbled off at rates that could not be excelled by automata. But if they did not always know what they were saying, they always meant it. If the service had been more intelligble, it would have been less emotional and edifying. There was not a sentiment, however incomprehensible, for which they were not ready to die or to damn.

Israel Zangwill
Jewish Prayer

Second Only to the Bible

Most rewarding is the glimpse into the soul of the Jewish people that one gains through an acquaintance with the siddur. In the prayers one can sense the pulse of the Jewish heart, the innermost feelings of the Jewish people in their moments of exaltation and dejection. One can also discern the Jewish people's aspirations and disillusionments, its ideals, and its profoundest beliefs. As a devotional compendium the siddur is characterized by its numerous supplications and beseechments directed to the God of Abraham, Isaac, and Jacob, its many utterances of gratitude to the Almighty for His blessings and His love, its repeated outpourings of grief over sins committed, and its unending expressions of confidence that the Father in heaven will in His compassion forgive Israel's transgressions and will restore His people to its former glory. Through the siddur one can also fathom the essence of Judaism and grasp "its strong doctrines of duty and righteousness, its moral earnestness, its cheery confidence in the world's possibilities of a sufficing and ennobling happiness, its faith in the purity and perfectibility of human nature, in brief, its ethical optimism." It is a treasure-house of prayers, hymns, psalms, affirmations of faith, and eternal hope. These vital characteristics have raised the siddur from the status of a useful handbook of worship to one of the most sacred books of Judaism, second only to the Bible.

Abraham Millgram
Jewish Worship

Why We Use the Prayer Book

There is yet another reason why man must speak. Until we have words, we do not even know what it is that we want to say. There is not first the content, and then the form into which this content is poured, but the form produces its own content. Human speech is not like medieval economics in which a man needed a pair of shoes, went to the shoe-maker and ordered them, and then the shoe-maker sat down and manufactured them. It is rather like modern commodity-production, in which the shoe-maker, having made the shoes, instigates the need for them on the part of the potential consumer. Congregations or individuals, left to their own devices, without prayer book or precentor, would know neither what to pray nor how to pray.

This is why we use the prayer book. One is asked: how do I learn to pray? There is really only one answer: pray!

Pray other people's prayers. You will appropriate them to yourself by using them and pouring your own personality into them. Do not wait until you "feel like" praying, or until you know how to pray. You never will. This is really a case of "we shall do and then hear." And even if we could occasionally speak without having to use the thoughts and words of others, how shabby and sentimentally self-indulgent such worship invariably turns out to be! "In a sense, our liturgy is a higher form of silence. . . . The spirit of Israel speaks, the self is silent."

Steven Schwarzschild
Judaism

The Prayer Book—The Property of Every Jew

The prayer book thus becomes the community's major contact with primary Jewish sources. Despite romantic notions to the contrary, it simply is not true that whole generations of Jews in the past have habitually been at home in the vast literature of the rabbis. Before the invention of printing, how many people could afford to possess even a few of the goodly number of books upon which the elaborate structure of rabbinic Judaism was constructed? And even after the Gutenberg revolution in typesetting, how many people had the leisure time, the intellectual ability, or the economic freedom to undertake serious study of a literature that had grown by leaps and bounds to include not only the two Talmuds but responsa from around the world, commentaries, midrash, philosophy, and several schools of mysticism.

But the prayer book was the property of every Jew. Before printing, people repeated prayers by rote, or at least listened to their recital daily. Wealthy patrons hired scribes to write personal copies of the siddur. And after the sixteenth century, the prayerbook was the one volume which made a crystallization of the Jewish legacy readily available. True, the literal meaning of the Hebrew words was often beyond the linguistic competence of Jews whose education was not what they might have wished, but the "message" inherent in the prayer book is transmitted by factors that go beyond comprehension of the prayers. That the prayer book owed its popularity to its unique capacity to carry such a vital message is beyond doubt.

Lawrence A. Hoffman
Gates of Understanding

We are like the child who does not know whether there is bread anywhere, but who cries out because he is hungry.

Simone Weil
Waiting for God

These Words Can Bring Us into the Presence of God

When we enter the synagogue and open our prayer books, we find words printed on paper. They can mean little or nothing, if so we are disposed. But the imaginative mind and the sensitive spirit and the intelligent heart may find tremendous power in these words . . . through them he will link himself to all the generations of his fathers in a golden chain of piety . . . he will join his fellows of the house of Israel everywhere, and time and space will be no hindrance as he pours out his soul together with his fathers and his brothers towards heaven. He will find words soothing and peaceful—and words rousing and challenging to the conscience.

But above all, these words, laden with the tears and joys of centuries, have the power to bring us into the presence of God. Not all at once, not easily, not every time: but somehow, sometime the faithful worshipers who take heart and soul into their hands and offer them up without reservation—somehow, sometime they will know that they have reached the throne of Glory, and that God has taken them by the hand.

Chaim Stern
Service of the Heart

Fundamental Jewish Beliefs Reflected in the Liturgy

The system of sacred duties which makes of Judaism a "portable religion" is buttressed and sustained by certain convictions which transform the Halakhah into a sacred access to God. These convictions are embedded and expressed in our liturgy. In this special sense, Judaism can be said to be a "liturgical religion," for its fundamental beliefs are most clearly reflected in its liturgy. In his prayers, the Jew gave voice to his yearning for God, to his deep sense of moral accountability, to his ecstatic love for the Torah, and to his invincible faith in his people's rehabilitation in a peaceful world. It was the liturgy in word (prayer) and in act (mitzvah) which gave our forebears high hope in the face of despair, and perseverance in the midst of persecution.

Max Arzt
Justice and Mercy

Unceasing Creative Power

The siddur is a world of prayer. It unites the Jews as a praying fellowship throughout the generations and the world, fostering in them what is finest and noblest. A source of ever-renewed inspiration and intimate communion with the Divine, it spans thousands of years and far-distant continents.

It links physical needs with spiritual longing. It leads from the finite and temporal to the infinite and eternal. Through it, God is no longer a distant abstraction, but becomes a vital reality. The Jew's daily companion, its creative power is unceasing.

R. Brasch
The Judaic Heritage

The Siddur Is of Paramount Importance

The Jewish prayer book, or the siddur, is of paramount importance in the life of the Jewish people. No other book in the whole range of Jewish literature that stretches over three millennia and more, comes so close to the life of the Jewish masses as does the prayer book. The siddur is a daily companion, and the whole drama of earthly existence—its joys and sorrows; workdays, Sabbath, historic and solemn festivals; birth, marriage and death—is sanctified by the formulae of devotion in that holy book. To millions of Jews, every word of it is familiar and loved; and its phrases and responses, especially in the sacred melodies associated with them, can stir them to the depths of their being. No other volume has penetrated the Jewish home as has the siddur; or has exercised, and continues to exercise, so profound an influence on the life, character and outlook of the Jewish people, as well in the sphere of personal religion as of moral character.

Joseph H. Hertz
The Jewish Prayer Book

The Old Prayer Book

The old tear-stained prayer book will
  I take in my hand
And call upon the God of my fathers
In my distress.
To the God of my fathers who was

their Rock and Refuge
In ages past,
I will pour out my woe
In ancient words, seared with the
pain
Of generations.
May these words that know the
heavenly paths
Bring my plaint to the God above,
And tell Him that which is hidden
in my heart—
What my tongue is incapable of
expressing.
These words, faithful and true, will
speak for me
Before God.
They will ask His pity.
And God in heaven who has heard
the prayers
Of my fathers,
The God who gave them power and
strength—
Perchance He will hear my prayer
too,
And my distress,
And will be a Shield unto me as He
was unto them.
For, like them, I am left a spoil unto
others,
Degraded and despised,
A wanderer over the face of the
earth.
And there is none who can help and
sustain me
Except God in heaven.

Yaakov Cohen
High Holiday Prayer Book

The Noblest Liturgy

When we come to view the half-dozen or so great Liturgies of the world purely as religious documents, and to weigh their values as devotional classics, the incomparable superiority of the Jewish convincingly appears. The Jewish Liturgy occupies its pages with the One Eternal Lord; holds ever true, confident, and direct speech with Him; exhausts the resources of language in songs of praise, in utterances of loving gratitude, in rejoicing at His nearness, in natural outpourings of grief for sin; never so much as a dream of intercessors or of hidings from His blessed punishments; and, withal, such a sweet sense of the divine accessibility every moment to each sinful, suffering child of earth. Certainly the Jew has cause to thank God, and the fathers before him, for the noblest Liturgy the annals of faith can show.

George E. Biddle
Jewish Quarterly Review

What the Prayer Book Gave to the Jew

The Greek word for prayer means "to wish for." The German word for prayer means "to beg." The English word means "to entreat, implore, ask earnestly or, supplicate, beg." The Hebrew word is *t'phila*. Its root is *pallal* which means "to judge." The act of praying in Hebrew is *hitpallel*, the reflexive form of the verb; it means "to judge oneself." It signifies self-examination, an inquiry into the state of one's soul, to make it ready for communication with God.

With reference to prayer, primitive minds regard themselves as serfs, and God as "the Lord of the manor," to whom one must constantly go begging for favors; flattering, cajoling, wheedling, obsequiously fawning—this is pagan prayer.

Jews look upon God as their Father and friend, in whose presence it is a delight to sit, with whom it is glorious and wonderful to converse. Whether as Father or as friend it were unseemly only to come into His presence to ask for something, begging.

Shneur Zalman of Liadi expressed the Jewish view when he interrupted his recitation of the set prayers in his siddur to say to God: "I do not want your paradise. I do not want your coming world. I want you and you only." This ecstatic exclamation is not written in any Jewish prayer book, but it is the inevitable response of a soul sensitized by constant reading of this prayer book, a reading that is not only of the eyes and the lips and vocal cords, but of the heart, of the soul itself.

Whenever Levi Yitzhak of Berditchev came to a certain passage of the liturgy he paused to talk with God thus: "Lord of the universe. I do not beg you to reveal to me the secret of your ways. I could not bear it: the burden of this knowledge. But show me one thing, show it to me more clearly and more deeply, show me what this which is happening to me at this very moment means to me, what it demands of me. What you, O Lord of the world, are telling me by way of it. Ah, it is not why I suffer that I wish to know, but only whether I suffer for your sake."

It was the frequent, almost constant use of his prayer book and the inspiration he not only got from it, but the inspiration he brought to it, that gave Levi Yitzhak and the host of pious Jews that enjoyed this same spiritual exercise in days that were less fortunate and materially less prosperous than ours—gave them this sense of a world drenched in divine light, shimmering and holy with the grace and the beauty of the Lord.

Albert S. Goldstein
Temple Bulletin

The Power of That Ancient Text

In the life of prayer we seek to create a constant awareness of the divinity that surrounds us at all times. We live in the divine presence as did our ancestors and as will our descendents. Prayer offers to the individual and the community something of an echo of eternity, and that single echo is borne by the multiple echoes of history and antiquity. It is for this reason that I believe the Hebrew language will remain a vital vehicle in the prayer life of the Jewish community. No translation bears for the Jewish soul even a faint reverberation of the tremendous power contained in the Hebrew liturgical text. We may not allow the power contained in that ancient text to be lost.

Arthur Green
The Reconstructionists

The Prayer Book Is Spiritual Training

Great religious and ethical influences were exercised by Judaism over the world through the Bible. But through the prayer book, also, it exercised an influence perhaps equally important. Whereas, through the Bible Judaism taught the world an ideal of religion nobler than any known before, through the prayer book and the Synagogue, it taught the world a mode of communion with God which made this noble religion liveable, intimate, and effective in daily life. The Bible is the meaning of Judaism; the prayer book, its method. The Bible is doctrine. The prayer book is spiritual training.

Solomon B. Freehof
The Small Sanctuary

A Potent Instrument of Survival

The siddur, as the Jewish prayer book is called in Hebrew, gives voice to the depth of Jewish faith. It is marked by an all-pervading and radiant optimism. It greets each new-born day with the ringing assertion that the soul with which God has endowed man is pure. It maintains an unyielding faith in the basic goodness of the human soul. A somber note is seldom heard.

The exiled Jew has trudged indeflectibly forward through the leaden footed centuries ever carrying joyously in his heart prayer for the regeneration of his people and the rebuilding of Zion. He has had an unwavering religious faith in the divine destiny that will override the man-made cataclysms of history. His prayer book has been for him a potent instrument of survival. In recurrent affirmations it promises that he will be comforted for the sorrows he has borne.

The prayers are irradiated by a glorious universalism and an unfailing vision of hope and betterment for all men. The Messianic concept of an ideal Golden Age is set not in the past but in the future. Blessings and prayers are addressed to God not only as our God and God of our fathers, but also to Him as *Avinu shebashamayim*, our Father who art in heaven, *Meleh haolam*, the King of the universe, and *Ribbono shel olam*, universal Lord.

The prayer book is a manual of intense personal devotion and piety; but it is no less the expression of Jewish social idealism. It voices the religious aspirations of the whole people and the aim to achieve an ennobled spiritual society. The prayers, overwhelmingly in the plural, express the striving of all the Jewish people to reach their God. In unifying brotherhood of worship the individual draws inspiration and strength from communal praying, while he brings to the congregation his increment of spiritual purpose and devotion.

David De Sola Pool
The Traditional Prayer Book

Our Liturgy Is a Higher Form of Silence

In a sense, our liturgy is a higher form of silence. It is pervaded by an awed sense of the grandeur of God which resists description and surpasses all expression. The individual is silent. He does not bring forth his own words. His saying the consecrated words is in essence an act of listening to what they convey. The spirit of Israel speaks, the self is silent.

Abraham Joshua Heschel
Man's Quest for God

To Warm Our Hands at the Fires Already Lighted

In prayer we must turn to the great religious geniuses, the Isaiahs and Jeremiahs and Psalmists, and make our own the visions they have seen, the communion they have established, the messages they have brought back, the words they have spoken as having been spoken for us because truly spoken for all men. And by an act of sympathetic fervor, of loving contagion, to achieve their glow, and to fan the spark which is present in all of us at the fire which they have lighted. This does not mean that all the deepest prayers and all the best poetry and all the highest music have all already been written, and that there is an end to inspiration. The future is open, there is no limitation on the wonder of insight and creation. But we each of us in our time and place have to husband the resources available and to warm our hands at the fires already lighted.

Henry Slonimsky
Prayer

Spiritual Discipline and Spiritual Growth

The siddur is a primary path to reliving the formative myths of the Jewish people, reviewing our key memories, reasserting our theology, reconnecting to community, and renewing our commitment to social justice. The siddur, however, is even more than that. It is an introduction to spiritual discipline and spiritual growth. The rhythms of ritual provide a powerful sense of the holy dimension in each day, week, month and year. The words of the siddur and the actions that accompany them create a ritual structure that enables us to sense the dimension of the holy. That ability becomes ours when we take on the aspirations, make commitments of time and energy, and discipline ourselves for the task.

David A. Teutsch
The Reconstructionist

The Prayer Book—A Jewish World

The sum and substance of the whole of historical Judaism, its handbook and its memorial tablet, will ever be the prayer book: the daily and the festival, the siddur and the machzor. He to whom these volumes are not a sealed book has more than grasped "the essence of Judaism." He is informed with it as with life itself; he has within him "a Jewish world."

Franz Rosenzweig
quoted by Nahum N. Glatzer in
Franz Rosenzweig, His Life and Thought

8 THE COLLECTIVE SOUL OF ISRAEL

God Does Not Despise the Prayer of the Many

The prayer of the congregation is always hearkened to, even if sinners are among them. God does not despise the prayer of the many, hence man should always join with the congregation in prayer. As long as he is able to pray with the congregation, he should not pray alone. He should go, morning and evening, to the synagogue, since prayer is only hearkened to at all times in the synagogue.

Moses Maimonides
Laws of Prayer

Prayer Begins with Self but Must Reach Out to All Mankind

Judaism may base its understanding of prayer on the individual man's relation to God, but it refuses to stop there. Judaism does not think of man abstracted from his relation to mankind. It does appreciate the meaning of the individual in isolation, but holds him, the single one, in unremitting importance, against a background of society and history. For the Jew, man is a social and historical creature. Hence his prayer should properly be a communal, comradely affair. Public worship is a universal human need and, also, a specifically Jewish requirement.

A religion which denied the worth of history might well consider private prayer superior to group prayer. But Judaism's basic view of the universe is historical. The Bible knows man almost from his creation as a child of history. Man's sin began and still powers the movement of events. But history is no senseless, chance succession. There is a God who rules over time. History has a purpose and a goal—that era when God's rule will be fully established by its manifestation in lives of justice, peace, and love. God's kingdom-to-be is not a private matter between one individual and God. It must be accomplished with all men and be manifest in all lives, or it is unworthy of the Lord of the universe. The individual man cannot understand himself, cannot properly know his own life's purpose unless he sees it within the context of all mankind and all of history. Isolated from his fellows, he isolates himself from God's social goals.

To want to pray, but only alone and only for oneself, seems therefore to make too much of self, too little of God. Judaism commends communal prayer because God cares for all as He cares for each one, because, while God is the God of each private individual, He is the God of *all* individuals as well. The single self is indispensable. Without any *one,* mankind is incomplete. So too, without *all other selves,* equally precious to God, the single self loses its context and hence its final significance. Man cannot find himself only in others, but he also cannot find himself without them. If prayer is supposed to open man to the truth of his existence it must begin with self but it must reach out to all mankind.

Judaism values communal worship not for its specific Jewish purposes alone, but for all men. Group prayer, by confronting us with others, by asking us to link our prayers to theirs, reminds us immediately and directly that it is never enough to pray for ourselves alone. Speaking as "we," the individual discovers, acknowledges, articulates the needs, desires, hopes, which he, though one man, shares with all men because he is not only a private self but a member of humanity. Besides, when we are conscious of those with whom we stand, what we may have wanted to pray by ourselves is generally made less selfish, more humble, and therefore more appropriate for utterance before God. There before us is the newly bereaved young widower with his three small children. Near him stand the white-haired man who, close to the age of retirement, suddenly faces bankruptcy; the beautiful young woman who has just come from the hospital after the removal of a breast; the quiet mother whose consultation with the school psychologist was deeply disturbing. When we join *them* in prayer, when we must, to say "we," link ourselves with them, we, and our prayer, are refined; and often exalted far beyond our own means, for *they are praying now,* lifting us, helping us, with their "we," even as they silently reach out to the congregation for compassion and understanding.

Eugene B. Borowitz
Gates of Understanding

When the Jew Is Never Alone

Communal worship made it possible to note the major occasions of a person's life. An individual's grief was shared by the congregation. So were his joys. The communal service was even tailored in parts to reflect the special occasion of one's personal life. Jews may have known much suffering, known too the empty feeling of being a people isolated in the world, but a Jew who regularly worshiped with a congregation was never alone.

Hayim Halevy Donin
To Pray as a Jew

We Want to Live On as a Jewish Community

Recently a colleague asked the question: "How is it permitted for us to pray 'Zachraynu l'chayim'—'remember us to life'—when we know that in the nature of things a time must come when that prayer cannot possibly be answered? God cannot always give us another year of life. Many offered that prayer last year who are no longer with us this year." As I thought about his question it occurred to me that when we ask "Zachraynu l'chayim," we are not asking for ourselves at all. The prayer is worded in the plural. We are asking for more than personal continuity. We are asking for the continuity of the Jewish people, of the congregation with which we pray. We want to live on as a Jewish community.

Now, a Jewish community can surrender a great deal and still remain Jewish but I don't think we can give up the habit of prayer and still remain a vital congregation. In order for us to survive we have to engage in the most distinctive Jewish activity—communal worship. If we pray for Jewish survival—"Zachraynu l'chayim"— we have to live in such a way to commit ourselves individually to participate with the congregation in worship.

Sidney Greenberg
Hidden Hungers

There Is a Special Quality to Group Prayer

Our sages taught that when one witnesses lightning, comets, thunder, hurricanes, or the like, he should pray, "Blessed is He whose almighty power fills the world." The same men who found the evidence of God everywhere taught the value of the formal prayer. A man can pray well and deeply when he finds God for himself through nature or through spiritual reflection, but there is another profound meaning of prayer when it is performed in association with other human beings who have come together with the avowed intention of searching as a group for the deeper meaning of life. Clinical psychological tests clearly show that a decision reached by a group can be more binding on each of the participants than a decision reached by an individual acting alone. There are decisions to be made when one is alone, and there are decisions which are best made by the group. Anyone who has felt the warmth and good-fellowship present at a congregational service, anyone who has witnessed the sharing of sorrow at a funeral, or the sharing of joy at a wedding, knows that there are things best accomplished in a group situation. The man who feels that he cannot reach God when he is alone is lacking in probing powers which must be trained and sharpened, but the person who feels that he does not need to share the aspirations and moods of the group is deceiving himself. Rabbi Mikhal prayed, "I join myself to all of Israel, to those who are more than I, that through these my thought may rise, and to those who are less than I, so that they may rise through my thought." There is a special quality to group prayer from which all men can benefit.

Our Sages taught that God proclaimed, "He who prays with a congregation is credited with redeeming Me and My children." This teaching reflects the strong Jewish conviction against the fragmentation of the community by those who flee from community responsibility and insist that they can gain nothing from the group. He who wishes to serve God cannot do so merely by staying out of trouble. He can "redeem" God only by working and praying with the community.

Our Sages also taught that certain prayers such as the "K'dushah, Sanctification" should not be recited by the individual alone. They were properly recited only in a group. Why did they come to this conclusion? Scripture teaches, "I will be hallowed among the children of Israel," (i.e., not by one child, not by an individual alone, but by the group acting in concert).

In this day, when there are strong pressures upon men to "go it" alone, we need the Synagogue more than ever. Our fathers were wise enough to know that when men pray together, they are less apt to engage in flights of fancy; they are less apt to pray selfishly; and they are the more easily reminded of their covenantal task. When men pray only when they are alone, they are not able to recite meaningfully the prayer which comes as the climax of our religious service, "Fervently we pray that day may come when all men . . . created in Thine image, shall recognize that they are brethren . . ." (*Union Prayerbook*, p. 71). The ultimate goal of prayer is to unite the hearts of men. Indeed our prayer book reads, "Unite our hearts, that we may serve thee *in truth*."

Herbert M. Baumgard
Judaism and Prayer

The King's Wish

Of communal prayer it has been told:

Once in a tropical country, a certain splendid bird,
more colorful than any that had ever been seen,
was sighted at the top of the tallest tree.
The bird's plumage contained within it
all the colors in the world.
But the bird was perched so high
that no single person
could ever hope to reach it.

When news of the bird reached the ears of the king,
he ordered that a number of men

try to bring the bird to him.
They were to stand on one another's shoulders
until the highest man could reach the bird
and bring it to the king.
The men assembled near the tree,
but while they were standing
balanced on one another's shoulders,
some of those near the bottom
decided to wander off.
As soon as the first man moved,
the entire chain collapsed,
injuring several of the men.
Still the bird remained uncaptured.

The men had doubly failed the king.
For even greater than his desire to see the bird
was his wish to see his people
so closely joined to one another.

Or Ha-Hochmah 4:31b–32a
Arthur Green
Barry Holtz
Your Word Is Fire

A Jew Is Never by Himself in Prayer

Judaism is fully aware of the religious inspiration which one may derive from confronting God in the solitude of one's most personal sorrow or joy; but Jews are able to derive no less inspiration from standing before God in the midst of the community. The intimacy of the confrontation with God may become even more real for a Jew for seeking His nearness together with other Jews. What the stillness of approaching God alone may do for other people, the waves of the praying voices of the community may do for a Jew. This is due to that specific quality of Jewish religiosity that we have discussed. The most singularly personal aspect of the piety of a Jew is significant because it remains within the context of the religious faith, the affirmations and commitments, of all Israel. A Jew, who overwhelmed by the mystical grandeur of God's creation falls on his knees and worships the Creator, is engaged in a act of individual piety. However, if he does so as an individual, without the realization that it is "our God and God of our fathers" whom he worships, without incorporating in his personal experience a sense of unity with the Jews of all ages who worshiped the same God before him, his individual piety is not Jewish. It is bound to have a quality which, from the religious point of view, will prove to be un-Jewish. All individual piety among Jews is validated by the closeness of its contact with the strivings and experiences of the people of God in all ages. Individual piety in Judaism has two roots: in the soul of the individual and in the soul of all Israel. Because of that, a Jew is never by himself in prayer. At the most lonely moments of his life, if he prays as a Jew, he prays with other Jews, with all the Jews who ever prayed before him and with all those who still pray. In a very palpable sense, Jewish praying is one. Every individual Jew, even if he is all by himself with his Maker, prays with all other Jews; every community of praying Jews is united in prayer with all other communities; and all communities of any single generation are linked by Jewish prayer to all the communities of all generations that ever approached God in prayer. It is for this reason that communal prayer may bring a Jew an original freshness of experience and depth of devotion which purely personal praying may never grant him. *T'filat Tsibbur* is really one prayer; it is the prayer of one people; it is the individual prayer of a people.

Eliezer Berkovits
Studies in Torah Judaism

The Great Worth of Congregational Worship

The institution of congregational worship is one of the great Jewish contributions to mankind. To be sure, a man can worship privately and can order his devotional life within the framework of his God-given personality. But the rabbis felt that the Jew who worships privately treads a spiritually lonely road. He lacks the spiritual uplift that one gains from corporate worship. The rabbis therefore taught that prayer is most efficacious when offered with a congregation. They interpreted the verse "But as for me, let my prayer be unto Thee, O Lord, in an acceptable time" (Psalm 69:14) to mean "when the congregation prays" (Berachot 7b–8a). One of the sages said that God's presence is in the synagogue, "for it is said: 'God standeth in the congregation of God' (Psalm 82:1)" (Berachot 6a).

It often happens that congregational services distract the worshiper from devotional concentration, or kavvanah. Occasionally, one is tempted to converse with his neighbor, especially when the service is not sufficiently decorous. Nonetheless, the rabbis preferred congregational to private prayer. One obvious reason is that it permits one to participate in a number of essential prayers which can be recited only at a group service. Another is that it enables one to participate in the instructional part of the service which is a central feature of Jewish worship. One can follow the reading of the scriptural portions and can listen to the religious discourse.

But more noteworthy is the psychological factor. A person who worships with a congregation derives much spiritual strength from sharing his experiences with the group. Corporate worship sustains the weak and supports the wavering. It enables one to pray with heightened devotion and greater kavvanah.

For the Jew, group worship has the added value of fusing more firmly his tie with the community of Israel. At a public service the Jew experiences a tangible association with his people, an experience which tends to rivet the links that bind him with Israel. Only in the synagogue does the Jew experience fully that feeling of commonality, that warmth of association, and that sentiment of belonging which strengthen his identification with the Jewish people.

The creation of a strong feeling of identity with the Jewish people is especially important to the Jew because his people is scattered abroad and constantly exposed to the pressures of the dominant non-Jewish cultures. These pressures usually cause a spiritual and cultural erosion which threatens the Jewish people with total disintegration. Congregational worship thus assumes a significance which transcends the devotional needs of the individual Jew; it is also an effective weapon in the Jew's eternal battle for survival.

Abraham Millgram
Jewish Worship

The Liberating Power of Public Worship

Public worship aids us by liberating our personality from the confining walls of the individual ego. Imprisoned in self, we easily fall a prey to morbid brooding. Interference with our career, personal disappointments and disillusionments, hurts to our vanity, the fear of death—all these tend so to dominate our attention that our minds move in a fixed and narrow system of ideas, which we detest but from which we see no escape. With a whole wide world of boundless opportunities about us, we permit our minds, as it were, to pace up and down within the narrow cell of their ego-prison. But participation in public worship breaks through the prison of the ego and lets in the light and air of the world. Instead of living but one small and petty life, we now share the multitudinous life of our people. Against the wider horizons that now open to our ken, our personal cares do not loom so large. Life becomes infinitely more meaningful and worthwhile, when we become aware, through our participation in public worship, of sharing in a common life that transcends that of our personal organism.

A sense of common consecration to ideals inherited from a distant past and projected into a remote future means that we have in a sense made ourselves immortal. For death cannot rob our life of significance and value to us so long as we are interested in passing on to our posterity a heritage of culture and ideals. The past before we were born and the future after our death are a part of us, and every moment is eternal that embraces them. Through our worship as part of a religious community that outlives all its members, this sense of our life's triumph over death and all manner of frustration is brought home to us. We thus experience an expansion of our personality, an enlargement of the scope of its interests and its capacities. It is as though by surrendering our souls to God, we admit God into our souls and partake of His infinity and eternity.

Mordecai M. Kaplan
The Meaning of God

The Special Benefits of Public Prayer

There are times when the religious individual wants to be alone with himself and with God. Some of our most meaningful prayers come at such times. But there are special benefits also to be derived from public collective prayer. When we worship together with others we counteract the feeling of futility and helplessness which so often afflicts every sensitive individual. We reinforce our identification with our fellowmen. We strengthen our belongingness within humanity, as a step toward perceiving how we belong, all of us together, to the universe and to life. When all is said and done, a primary purpose of prayer for each of us must be to enlarge his horizons. Both his human and his cosmic horizons. Perhaps this is why the Talmud enjoins: "Pray only in a room with windows."

This is also, I think, something of what Martin Buber means: "To begin with oneself, but not to end with oneself; to start from oneself, but not to aim at oneself; to comprehend oneself, but not to be preoccupied with oneself."

Roland Gittelsohn
Man's Best Hope

The Sanctity We Feel in the Social Bond

Public worship draws out the latent life in the spirit of man. Those who, when alone, do not, or cannot, pray, find an impulse to prayer when they worship with others; and some will pray together who cannot pray alone, as many will sing in chorus who would not sing solos. As two walking together in some dark wood feel stronger and braver each for the other's near presence, so many who are spiritually weak in themselves will find spiritual strength in a common spiritual effort. That is the value of public worship for the individual. It has also a social value.

Public worship expresses the sanctity we feel in the social bond. A congregation at worship is a society declaring its devotion to God, a fellowship of men forged by faith in Him. Here is an experience that can deepen the social spirit and strengthen the bond of sympathy among men. If in public worship we realise that my prayers are also the prayers of the man who is by my side, it will make us more effectively aware of our common humanity and implant a spirit which will be potent for social good. They who worship God together bring Him into their mutual relations. If public worship does not produce this result, then it is but private worship in a public place. If it does bring men closer together under the influence of God, then it is a way to the sanctification of human society.

Israel I. Mattuck
Service of the Heart

We Stand before God in the Company of Our People

When a Jew prays, it is not as though a finite human being suddenly took it into his head that he may attune his mind to the infinite mind of God. Rather can he build, as it were, upon the contact which had been established long, long ago. The faith community of Israel today stands in prayer before the God of Israel even as it has stood before Him ever since Sinai, and even as its Patriarchs, Abraham, Isaac and Jacob, had already turned to Him when our people was as yet but a single tribal family. The prayer I address to "our God and God of our fathers, God of Abraham, God of Isaac, and God of Jacob" is indeed the prayer which *I* offer; but it is also a strand within that tapestry of prayer woven by generations upon generations of my ancestors, and joined to those many other strands which my fellow Jews in all parts of the world are contributing at this very moment. In other words, standing before God in prayer, I do not stand alone. I stand in the company of my people, a company both visible and invisible, spanning space as well as time.

Community prayer, then, adds another dimension to prayer, a dimension which is not accessible to him who would go off alone into the woods to commune with God in nature. It certainly does not invalidate such individual prayer. It supplements it. And for many, although perhaps not for all, it makes prayer itself easier. It helps to make manifest the presence of the Holy One, whom the psalmist describes as "enthroned upon the praises of Israel" (Psalm 22:4).

Jakob J. Petuchowski
Dynamics and Doctrine

Pray with the Congregation in Hebrew

In our times, since no one is capable of translating Hebrew with absolute accuracy, even one who does not understand Hebrew well and wants to say the service in another language, is admonished not to separate himself from the ways of the community. It is the custom of all Jewish communities from time immemorial to say the prayer service only in Hebrew.

One can fulfill his obligation even if he does not understand the service. . . . He can easily learn the general meaning of the prayers, even if he doesn't understand each word. If even this is too difficult, he should still pray with the congregation in Hebrew. He can later repeat the service in any other language that he understands.

Efraim Zalman Margolioth of Brody
Bet Efraim

Abaye said: One should always include himself with the community. He should therefore say, "May it be Your will, O God our Lord, that You bring *us* in peace. . . ."

Berachot 29b–30a

We Are Part of the Fellowship of Israel

Public worship generally is an occasion when we proclaim that we are part of the fellowship of Israel in covenant with God. The prayer book is liturgical agada. Its words are designed to evoke, express, confirm that we individuals—with all the personal agendas and histories which distinguish us from each other—share a common story that is the key to our life's transcendent meaning. The peak moments of authentic worship are moments when we feel that the words of Moses to the children of Israel, or of Jacob to his sons, are words addressed to us. Liturgical agada is the language through which the children of Israel in each generation reaffirm the covenant of their fathers.

Samuel E. Karff
Agada: The Language of Jewish Faith

Public Worship Makes One Feel at Home in the World

Participation in public worship makes one feel at home in the world. In our efforts to maintain and preserve our individuality, we are too often aware of our natural and social environment by the resistance it offers to these efforts. This makes us feel lonely and forsaken, as though we were marooned on an island inhabited by a strange and savage people, with only our individual resources of body and mind on which to depend. The odds then seem so tremendously against us that it hardly appears worthwhile to struggle with our fate. The responsibilities of life are too burdensome, unless we are aware of a supporting and sustaining power outside our individual selves on which we can count. This awareness is present when we find ourselves in the fellowship of others who have similar interests, acknowledge similar responsibilities, and respond appreciatively to similar values. Realizing that others share our needs, our hopes, our fears, and our ideals we no longer feel dependent entirely on our own efforts for our salvation. A trickle of water cannot move a mill-wheel, but when these trickles flow together and become a gushing torrent they can. The presence of others participating with us in articulating our common ideals assures us that we are not separate drops of water, but parts of the mighty current of human life.

Even this is inadequate to explain the effect of public worship on the spirit of the individual worshiper. Two ship-wrecked men in a row-boat on an angry sea have more than twice the chance of saving themselves than each would have in a boat for himself. Not only can each count on the strength of the other, but, not being alone, he is less likely to be stupefied by fear. He himself, therefore, by reason of the companionship, becomes more resourceful, steadier and more efficient in his rowing. The presence of a comrade thus enables him to discover and take advantage of circumstances favorable to his saving himself, which would otherwise in his panic have escaped his notice. The presence of a friend in the boat, makes even nature seem more friendly, more capable of responding to his needs. He is more aware that, not only in man but in man's natural environment he has invisible allies on whose help he can count: his oars, his boat itself, the remainder of his food and water supply, a favorable wind or current, and somewhere within reach, if his efforts can hold out long enough, the hospitable shore or a rescuing ship. Thus public worship not only enhances our strength by its suggestion of human cooperation, but by banishing morbid fear it gives us renewed confidence in nature itself, enabling us to see in it as well as in humanity the immanence of God. Thus public worship makes us feel not only that we have brothers on earth, but that we also have—to use the traditional metaphor—a Father in heaven, a Power in nature that responds to human need, if properly approached.

Mordecai M. Kaplan
The Meaning of God

Jews Assembled in Prayer Are a Miniature National Assembly

Judaism is not a religion of individual souls but that of a people. This again is due to the fact that Judaism is not a creed in the sense that one should be saved by faith alone; in Judaism one must implement one's belief and one's deeds. The deed, however, is life in its entirety, and life in its entirety is never life in isolation, not even that of the individual. The whole of life, in all its manifestations, personal or political, ethical or economical, individual or social must be lived with the awareness that it is being enacted by man in the presence of God. This is not a task for an individual, but for mankind as a whole; and until such time when mankind as a whole may embrace the responsibility, it will be realizable only by "a smaller mankind," a people that is committed to the aspiration of living its life as a people in the Sight of God. One may believe in Judaism as an individual, one can live as a Jew only together with other Jews. It is in this sense that Judaism is the religion of a people. It is the way of life of a whole people; it is the way of life that has determined the essential quality of a people. In Judaism it is not only the individual that confronts God; the people as a people is committed to living in such confrontation. As it lives as a people in the presence of God so it turns to God in prayer as a people. This is specifically Jewish. *T'filat tsibbur* is not congregational prayer; every *minyan* is an *eidah*, because it signifies the whole of Israel. Jews assembled in prayer are not a congregation but a miniature national assembly at prayer.

Eliezer Berkovits
Studies in Torah Judaism

Communal Prayer Has Many Advantages

Communal prayer has many advantages. In the first instance a community will never pray for a thing which is harmful to the individual whilst the latter sometimes prays for something to the disadvantage of other individuals, or some individuals may pray for something that is to *his* disadvantage. It has been laid down, therefore, that the individual recite the prayers of a community . . . so that one makes up for the forgetfulness or error of the other. In this way complete prayer is gained, its blessing resting on everyone. . . . A person who prays but for himself is like one who retires alone into his house refusing to assist his fellow citizens in the repair of the walls. His expenditure is as great as his risk. He, however, who joins the majority spends little, yet remains in safety because one replaces the defects of the other.

Yehuda Halevi
The Kuzari

Personal Prayer Can Be Strengthened by Public Prayer

Personal prayer can be strengthened by praying with a *minyan*. The impact of a *minyan* upon the depth and meaningfulness of personal prayer was brought home to me by the *minyan* I was permitted to organize in the sickroom of Franz Rosenzweig nearly thirty years ago. Rosenzweig was already too ill to leave his room. He could no longer move around and was immobilized in his chair. Several days before Rosh Hashanah I asked him whether he wanted a small group of friends to conduct a holiday service for him in his home. He eagerly consented. We conducted services on both days of Rosh Hashanah in Rosenzweig's room. The next day he asked, in the only way in which he could still communicate—by pointing his finger in the direction of certain letters on the typewriter while his wife attempted to guess what he meant—"What about Shabbat Shuvah?" We continued our *minyan*, first on Shabbat Shuvah, then on Yom Kippur, and from then on every Shabbat and holiday until his death. It was a good *minyan*. It taught us how to pray. The *minyan* had not been organized for this purpose, yet one of its by-products was that it taught many of us to pray.

Rosenzweig was too ill to pronounce the berachah over the Torah audibly. Nevertheless, we often called him to the Torah and then brought the Torah over to him. Rarely can a benediction have been said with such power, vigor, and kavvanah as was the silent benediction which Rosenzweig pronounced while bending his noble head.

Ernst Simon
Tradition and Contemporary Experience

Prayer Molds Community Conscience

Prayer is the most intensely personal expression of the human soul. But just as in the Psalms, so in the general prayers of the Synagogue, the individual worshiper immerses his individuality in the collective soul of Israel. No mediator is permitted to stand between the worshiper and Him to whom worship is directed. But granting some exceptions of prayers of an individual character, the chief prayers are designed for the individual as a member of a human brotherhood, or the household of Israel.

As the Jew bows in prayer before the Lord God, King of the universe, and pours out his heart before "the God of our Fathers, the God of Abraham, Isaac, and Jacob" he no longer stands before his Maker as a naked soul but as a social personality with hallowed memories. The contents of the prayers are cast in the collective plural. The worshiper in the Synagogue prays not for himself alone but for the common welfare. Petition, in general, is but a small part of the Synagogue prayers. Adoration, praise, and thanksgiving form the major theme of the Hebrew prayers and all living creatures are invoked to raise their voice in songs and hymns of glory. Although prayers may be recited in the home and when "thou walkest by the way," it is believed that they find greater merit when uttered in unison with other worshipers. Some themes, such as the *Kaddish*, the exalted prayer for the coming of the kingdom of God, are to be recited only when there is a quorum of at least ten male worshipers assembled. Through these and other subtle psychological suggestions, the Synagogue utilized the mystic power of prayer to foster the feeling of social responsibility and community conscience.

Abraham A. Neuman
Landmarks and Goals

The Jew Stands before God as a Member of the Community

It is not safe to pray alone. Tradition insists that we pray with, and as a part of, the community; that public worship is preferable to private worship. Here we are faced with an aspect of a *polarity of prayer*. There is a permanent union between individual worship and community worship, each of which depends for its existence upon the other. To ignore their *spiritual symbiosis* will prove fatal to both.

How can we forget that our ability to pray we owe to the community and to tradition? We have learned how to pray by listening to the voice of prayer, by having been a part of a community of men standing before God. We are often carried toward prayer by the reader: when we hear how he asks questions, how he implores, cries, humbles himself, sings.

Those who cherish genuine prayer, yet feel driven away from the houses of worship because of the sterility of public worship today, seem to believe that private prayer is the only way. Yet, the truth is that private prayer will not survive unless it is inspired by public prayer. The way of the recluse, the exclusive concern with personal salvation, piety in isolation from the community, is an act of impiety.

Judaism is not only the adherence to particular doctrines and observances, but primarily living in the spiritual order of the Jewish people, the living *in* the Jews of the past and *with* the Jews of the present. Judaism is not only a certain quality in the souls of the individuals, but primarily the existence of the community of Israel. It is not a doctrine, an idea, a faith, but the covenant between God and the people. Our share in holiness we acquire by living in the Jewish community. What we do as individuals is a trivial episode; what we attain as Israel causes us to become a part of eternity.

The Jew does not stand alone before God; it is as a member of the community that he stands before God. Our relationship to Him is not as an I to a Thou, but as a We to a Thou.

Abraham Joshua Heschel
Man's Quest for God

The Language of Prayer—A Living Link

Setting down the text of prayers in Hebrew was not only for the benefit of those who understood the language, but for the entire Jewish people. It was done to implant in the heart of every Jew, wherever he might be, the knowledge that he belonged to the Children of Israel, and to make him feel that he shared in their cultural history. The language of prayer is a living link between scattered Jewry, while the setting down of the texts perpetuated the language and ensured that it should not be forgotten by the masses of the Jewish people.

Abraham Kon
Prayer

Praying with the Congregation

One of the most effective instruments for preserving the Jewish consciousness is public worship. . . . The service of the Synagogue is something more than an expression of the needs and emotions of the individual worshippers who take part in it. It is an expression of the joys and sorrows, a proclamation of the hopes and ideals of Israel. . . . For the Synagogue is the one unfailing well-spring of Jewish feeling. There we pray together with our brethren, and in the act become participators in the common sentiment, the collective conscience, of Israel. There we pray with a mightier company still, with the whole house of Israel. We become members of a far greater congregation than that of which we form a physical part. We join our brethren in spirit all over the world in their homage to the God of our people. Under its influence our worship acquires a deeper fervor, a heightened dignity; our attachment to Israel is strengthened.

Morris Joseph
Judaism as Creed and Life

Like New Water

Rabbi Judah said in the name of Rabbi Meir: Just as new water constantly flows from the well, so Israel constantly utters a new song, as it is written: "And whether they sing or dance, all my thoughts are in Thee" (Psalm 87:7).

Midrash Shohar Tov on Psalms

Private Prayer and Public Prayer

A Synagogue service cannot evoke that which does not exist. A congregation composed of people who do not follow discipline of prayer in their personal lives cannot expect to generate an atmosphere congenial to worship and communion with God. Our public services can only move individuals who pray at home or when alone. We shall not make public worship more inspiring and elevating by devising additional aids or introducing new melodies. We will have spiritually enriching and emotionally satisfying services when the men and women who come to worship are not unacquainted with prayer in their private lives.

Do you really wish to have Synagogue services become more meaningful? Begin praying at home. Recite a blessing at the beginning of your family meal and a short prayer at the end. Start the day with a prayer, however brief, and retire at night only after an expression of gratitude to God for the gifts of life, love, health and freedom. After a time, you will find, that when next you attend a service, you will experience religious devotion and interest in praying with the Congregation.

Morris Adler
Shaarey Zedek Recorder

Congregants Must Participate

Without individuals investing their thoughts and emotions, their full attention, their devoted selves, in prayer, the Jewish service has lost its meaning. Whenever one "listens to" the rabbi or cantor, more in peaceful enjoyment than in identification and common meaning, the crucial distinction between the synagogue and the recital hall has been transgressed. Once started on this passive way, the congregation will always find it easier to shift its prayer responsibilities to those whom it has hired to pray for it. They do it so nicely, so dependably. They should really be allowed to do it all—which is but one step from having them do it alone, without benefit of congregants, not just participating but even attending. The rabbi and the cantor must be masters of their craft if they are to lead their congregants, yet they must use their talents to stimulate, not replace individual participation if they are to keep their services Jewish at their core.

Jewish worship is by belief and practice uncompromisingly individualistic, and its future depends upon the increasing ability of individual Jews to participate in the service and fulfill its expectations.

Eugene B. Borowitz
Rediscovering Judaism

Angels Convert Prayers into a Crown for God

When Israel prays, they do not all pray at once. Rather every congregation prays by itself, first one then another. After all the congregations furnish all the prayers, the angel that oversees prayer takes all the prayers that were said in all the synagogues, and makes them into a crown, and places them on the head of the Holy One Blessed be He.

Exodus Rabbah 21:4

Why Ten?

It is written (that when Abraham was arguing with God to save Sodom, he said) (Genesis 18:32), "What if there be ten there?" and God said, 'I will not destroy it for the sake of the ten.'" Why ten? In order that they all form a congregation. . . .

Genesis Rabbah 49:13

To Include the Community

One who only prays for his own needs is like one who works to strengthen his house alone, and does not want to help the people of his land strengthen the walls (of the city). Even though he expends much effort he remains in danger. But one who includes himself with the community, expends little, and remains safe.

Yehuda Halevi
The Kuzari

What I Learned from My Mother's Prayers

I cherish childhood memories of how my mother prayed during the synagogue service. It was very moving to listen to the way she spoke with such feelings of loving intimacy with God. In the midst of the service, I could hear her asking God to ensure that her adult sons would find good brides and that her husband would be able to support his family with dignity. Her prayers gave expression to her personal yearnings as a wife and mother. Her language was in no way inhibited or stunted. As I listened to her prayers, I did not sense that she felt unworthy to approach God with "petty" personal needs. She would have been astonished if someone had told her that the significance of prayer is to manifest an Akedah consciousness and asked how she dared feel so relaxed and easy before God. My mother, a deeply traditional Jew, prayed in the manner of generations of Jewish mothers. She continued a tradition that she received from her own family.

From my mother's prayers, I learned that commitment to structure and form does not necessarily inhibit personal expression. The personal and intimate can live within the structured formal framework of halakhic liturgy. Both together have always been part of the Judaic experience of prayer. The communal dimension is made possible through having a fixed language and appointed times for the service. The tradition endowed this aspect of prayer with seriousness, not because it believed that prayer becomes possible only through sacrificing one's own personal identity, but because halakhic Jews do not stand before God only as single individuals. They include the community in the life of worship. The community as a whole enters into the covenant of *mitzvah*, and in the prayer experience the individual Jew gives expression to his or her covenantal communal consciousness. Centrality of the community, however, was never meant to negate or crush the individual's natural impulse to pray.

The two distinct legitimizations of prayer in the Babylonian Talmud (Berachot 26b)—"Prayers were instituted by the patriarchs" and "Prayers were instituted to replace the daily sacrifices"—exemplify the combination of the individual and communal dimensions in Judaic prayer. By relating the prayer service to the sacrifices of the temple, the rabbis provided a framework for the ongoing drama of communal worship even after the destruction of the temple. The morning and afternoon sacrifices had been communal in nature. They had provided a symbolic form in which the total community could recognize that it stood as a unit before God. The motif that prayer replaces sacrifice is an attempt to keep the former communal consciousness alive in the prayer experience, since the liturgy, too, provides a structure for the total community to stand as one before God. The motif that prayer was initiated by the patriarchs, on the other hand, demonstrates the essential naturalness an individual Jew feels before God. The patriarchal experience reflects the role of the individual in prayer, whereas the memory of the sacrifices expresses the role of the community. The Talmud thereby unites both the individual and the communal dimensions of prayer. The two can live together. Neither need negate or repress the other.

The fixed petitional prayers express the fundamental needs of Israel as a total community. Through those prayers, the primacy of the community is established in each individual's consciousness. Simultaneously, however, the Talmud encourages individuals to bring their own individual requests before God during their recitation of those very same petitional prayers for the community. They express their personal needs before God within a structured liturgical framework that demonstrates their concern for the well-being of a total society. The communal dimension has the role of widening the range of individual consciousness, not the role of redeeming it from an exaggerated sense of nothingness and lack of worth. It is built, however, upon the dignity that individual Jews feel as worshipers who are encouraged by talmudic teachers to offer their own spontaneous prayers before God.

David Hartmann
A Living Covenant

Often a prayer is not heard until many people recite it together.

Nachman of Bratzlav
Sefer Ha-Middot

The Synagogue Is Unique

Great ideas and ideals must not be left suspended in imagination, but should be implemented in life. They must be symbolized and concretized in order to be properly understood and habitually practiced. Religion must of necessity be formalized in institutions. The supremacy of Judaism has come about with the creation and development of the synagogue, the institution which has incorporated the belief and meaning of One God; which has developed prayer, worship, study, social action, and righteous living. The synagogue as an institution is unique, with a long history and an interesting development. It has become the prototype for the Church and the Mosque. The synagogue is a living, growing, changing institution and not a relic of historical antiquity. It is one of the oldest, continuous, living religious institutions in human life. It may, at times, have its shortcomings, but it possesses enough vitality to overcome disintegrating forces. As in the past, it takes its place today as the living, universal Jewish institution.

Joshua Kohn
The Synagogue in Jewish Life

It is this merging with a congregation that makes prayer unselfish.

Moses Hasid
Iggeret Ha-Musar

The Contribution of the Synagogue

Prayer is, of course, not the invention of the synagogue. It is, to use the words of an old mystic, as natural an expression of the intimate relations between heaven and earth, as courtship between the sexes. Inarticulate whisperings, however, and rapturous effusion at far intervals are sometimes apt to degenerate into mere flirtations. The Synagogue, by creating something like a liturgy, appointing times for prayer, and erecting places of worship, gave steadiness and duration to these fitful and uncontrolled emotions, and raised them to the dignity of a proper institution.

Solomon Schechter
Studies in Judaism

What the Synagogue Has Meant and Means

1. The synagogue provides the ideal Jewish setting for worship, where that which is noblest within ourselves reaches out toward that which is highest in the universe—God.
2. The synagogue provides a place of assembly for the Jewish community and for the many organizations of Jewish youth and adults. It is the recognized address of the Jewish community for Jew and non-Jew alike.
3. The synagogue is the institution that best preserves the Jewish heritage and most effectively transmits the teachings of the prophets, the wisdom of our sages and teachers.
4. The synagogue has been the most potent force for Jewish continuity throughout the vicissitudes of our history. It continues to nourish the Jewish will to survive and to provide joy in living as a Jew.
5. The synagogue raises to loftiest significance the great milestones from birth to death by clothing them in the warmth of hallowed words and sacred rituals, and by providing a community with which to share these exalted occasions.
6. The synagogue keeps alive and articulates our people's most treasured memories, our most fervent beliefs and our most cherished hopes.
7. The synagogue provides a fellowship for Jews who take their heritage

seriously and who look to it to provide guidance, solace and inspiration.

8. The synagogue nurtures our faith in the coming of an era of peace and justice for all people, it gives us the courage to work for God's kingdom and the patience to hopefully wait for it.
9. The synagogue drapes each human being with highest dignity, confers upon life ultimate meaning, invests the universe with high purpose and sees in Jewish destiny cosmic significance.
10. The synagogue richly merits the tribute paid to it by Robert T. Herford, a Christian scholar: "In all their long history, the Jewish people have done scarcely anything more wonderful than to create the synagogue. No human institution has a longer continuous history, and none has done more for the uplifting of the human race."

Sidney Greenberg
The Philadelphia Inquirer

I Am the Synagogue

I am the heart of Jewry. I have sheltered you for more than two thousand five hundred years. Through all these cruel ages, swept by wrath of fire and sword, I nursed you with Word of God, healed your wounds with the balm of faith, steadied your minds and hearts with the vision of the Eternal.

When your fathers wept by the waters of Babylon, I came into the world, summoned by their need. In Persia, Greece and in Rome, in the face of the howling crusaders and in the clutches of the Black Inquisition, in the pogroms of Poland and in the concentration camps of the Nazis, I have been, and by my presence brought the living waters of the Eternal to the parched lips of your fathers.

I am old and I am young. I am older than the memories of the historians; and as young as the youngest child.

I bring you peace by teaching you duty. I sanctify your lives with holy seasons. I preserve your heritage. I make the faith of the father, the faith of the children. Behold, a good doctrine do I give unto you; forsake it not.

Author Unknown

The Dynamo of the Jewish Community

The historic synagogue is not only a *bet ha-t'filah,* "a house of prayer." It is also a *bet ha-k'neset,* "a house of assembly." Not only was it the gathering place for all Jewish communal discussions, but it also reflected the joys and sorrows of every Jew in the neighbourhood. When a male child was born, candles were lit in the synagogue on the eighth day when the boy was admitted to the "Covenant of Abraham." A baby girl was named when the father was called up to the reading of the Torah. A wedding took place near or in the synagogue, and special prayers were offered in the synagogue for the bride and groom on the Sabbath before the wedding. To this day mourners are welcomed with words of comfort on their entry into the synagogue at the inauguration of the Sabbath during the week of mourning. The wandering poor often ate and slept in the synagogue. When necessary, the synagogue became a people's court. A Jew who felt that he had a just grievance against another had the right to stop the reading of the Torah at the service until he gained a public promise of redress. And justly so! What value is there, otherwise, in reading the Law if the congregation will tolerate an injustice!

Besides serving as a house of prayer and a house of assembly, the historic synagogue had a third function. It was a *bet ha-midrash*, a "house of study." Where necessary it housed the local Talmud Torah, the elementary religious school. In all cases, the public opinion of the synagogue brought pressure upon every parent to arrange for the religious teaching of his children. The synagogue was the library and reading room of the community—institutions which were popular in Israel many centuries before modern communities realized their public value. But what was most important, men came daily to the synagogue to study individually and in groups. Rare, indeed, was a synagogue where the sound of Talmudic discussion was not heard and where there were no groups of men studying regularly the books of the Bible and of the rabbis, the thoughts of the prophets and the sages.

Thus the synagogue was the spiritual, the social, and the cultural reservoir and dynamo of the Jewish community. It was there that the Jewish will, head, and heart developed. There too the Jew developed the ideals and the strength of character which enabled him to survive on a high moral and cultural plane.

David Aronson
The Jewish Way of Life

The Democracy of the Synagogue

There is a democracy of prayer in Israel. Every Jew wears the *Tallit*. Every Jew who is able and worthy can lead the congregation in worship. It is not a sacrament reserved for a special body of anointed ones and denied to others. Even the last remnants of ancient aristocracy which remain within Israel, the *Kohanim* and *Leviim*, the descendents of the priests and levites, are so emptied of the normal accountrements of inherited nobility that they, too, strangely enough, often contribute an equalizing influence. It matters not how much wealth or influence a man may have, only a *Kohen* is called up first to the reading of the Torah.

There is an incident that occurs regularly in modern Israel which gives added meaning to this. In the most important synagogue in Jerusalem, in which the dignitaries of the city, including the President of the State of Israel, pray regularly, a strange event takes place. Each morning a slender, middle-aged Yemenite Jew, known as Yechezkel HaKohen (the priest), arrives punctually in the synagogue, goes to the closet, removes his work clothes—he is a street cleaner—puts on his only suit, takes part in the morning prayers, and at that point of the service when the priests bless the people (performed daily in Jerusalem), he ascends before the ark, covers his face with the long *Tallit*, stretches out his hands, and he, Yechezkel HaKohen, the humble street cleaner from the humble land of Yemen, blesses the great and dignified assemblage. After the service he returns to the closet, removes his only suit, hangs it up carefully, dresses in his work clothes again and leaves the sanctuary to begin his routine task of cleaning the filth from the streets of Jerusalem. For one minute each day he assumes the glories of the priests of old. The wise and the rich bow their heads before him, Yehezkel HaKohen, the street cleaner.

Samuel H. Dresner
Prayer, Humility, and Compassion

The Synagogue—A Unique Creation

A unique creation of Judaism is the Synagogue, which started it on its world-mission and made the Torah the common property of the entire people. Devised in the Exile as a substitute for the Temple, it soon eclipsed it as a religious force and a rallying point for the whole people, appealing through the prayers and Scriptural lessons to the congregation as a whole. The Synagogue was limited to no one locality, like the Temple, but raised its banner wherever Jews settled throughout the globe. It was thus able to spread the truths of Judaism to the remotest parts of the earth, and to invest the Sabbath and Festivals with deeper meaning by utilizing them for the instruction and elevation of the people. What did it matter, if the Temple fell a prey to the flames for a second time, or if the whole sacrificial cult of the priesthood with all its pomp were to cease forever? The soul of Judaism lived indestructibly in the House of Prayer and Learning.

Kaufmann Kohler
Jewish Theology

Where Can He Be Found?

Rabbi Joshua said: "The one who prays in his own house is, as it were, surrounded by an iron wall . . . the one who prays in the synagogue is regarded as having brought up a pure, meal offering. . . . 'Seek the Lord where He can be found' (Isaiah 55:6). Where can He be found? In the synagogue and houses of study."

Yerushalmi, Berachot 5:1

Jewish Living Needed for Jewish Praying

The only way to save the synagogue is by liquidating "Synagogue Judaism." The place of worship is not to be separated from the life that surges around its walls. The quality of worship is determined by the quality of the worshiper, which is moulded by forces outside the synagogue. These forces, if they are to create Jewish character, must be directed and applied by the spiritual strength of the living community. . . . Without practice outside the synagogue, there is no true devotion inside it. Without Jewish living, there can be no Jewish praying.

Eliezer Berkovits
Toward Historic Judaism

There Is Much Comfort in High Hills

By setting aside a place in which to worship, by repairing there frequently to replenish his spiritual powers, by learning there what his faith has to teach about life and its meaning, and by meeting there with like-minded fellows to encourage him and to strengthen him in his resolves, the Jew "ascends the mount of the Lord." He comes into contact with a world of elevated values and though he may soon come down to earth again he is the better for having been on the heights.

> There is much comfort in high hills,
> And a great easing of the heart.
> We look upon them, and our nature fills
> With loftier images from their life apart.
> They set our feet on paths of freedom, bent
> To snap the circles of our discontent.

The synagogue can do this for the modern Jew who learns, as his ancestors did, to revere it and make its ideal his own.

Louis Jacobs
Jewish Prayer

The Synagogue Adds Mysteriously . . .

Truly, God is everywhere. But to unite in worship in a building specially dedicated to this purpose not only adds mysteriously to the fervor of the individual worshipers but generates its own unequaled atmosphere of devotion. A worshiping community is as different from the same number of individuals praying apart as a bed of coals is from scattered cinders. The very existence of synagogues is a perpetual reminder of man's need and duty to pray. In addition, congregational worship creates a communal and historical consciousness.

R. Brasch
The Judaic Heritage

The Synagogue Nurtures the Eternal Vision

It is the synagogue which in every community stands as the witness to God, as the testimony of our faith that the world is not a meaningless accident, that there is a Power making for justice and mercy in the world, and that we live well only as we permit that Power to enter into our hearts, and to form our thoughts and deeds. The synagogue is the visible embodiment of the soul's irrepressible cry, "Oh Lord, our God, how glorious is Thy name in all the earth." It is in the synagogue that man is constantly admonished to meditate on the high purposes of his life. It is from the synagogue, yea, even from its mute walls, that there emanates daily into the thoughts and life of the body politic the admonition, "It is not by human might, and not by human power, but by the Divine spirit within us that man ultimately prevails. Thine, Oh Lord, is the greatness, the power, Thine are riches and honor and Thou art Sovereign over all." The synagogue nurtures within us the eternal vision of Father Jacob's dream, the vision of an earth joined to heaven, of a human society distinguished by its divine attributes, the vision of an earth in which no one shall have to flee from the wrath of his brother, for it shall be full of the knowledge of the Lord "as the waters cover the sea." That service the synagogue must be prepared to perform for us today as human beings, as Jews, and as citizens of America.

Simon Greenberg
Address to United Synagogue Convention, 1950

Judaism's Great Contribution

Judaism's greatest contribution to humanity is in the domain of public worship, where alone man develops the wings and the capacity to soar into an invisible world. This it made through the *synagogue*. The synagogue represents something without precedent in antiquity; and its establishment forms one of the most important landmarks in the history of Religion. It meant the introduction of a mode of public worship conducted in a manner hitherto quite unknown, but destined to become the mode of worship of civilized humanity.

Joseph H. Hertz
Daily Prayer Book

The Synagogue Kept Judaism Alive

Since the Middle Ages, the synagogue has been the visible expression of Judaism; it has kept the Jew in life, and enabled him to survive to the present day. With a truer application than that made by Macaulay in his day, we may declare that the synagogue, like the Ark in Genesis, carried the Jew through the deluges of history, and that within it are the seeds of a nobler and holier human life, of a better and higher civilization.

Joseph A. Hertz
Daily Prayer Book

The Influence of the Synagogue

To the Jews . . . the synagogue was a place for instruction in the truths and duties of revealed religion; and in imparting and receiving this divine instruction no less than in praise or prayer they were doing honor to God—it was an act of worship. The consequence of the establishment of such a rational worship for the whole subsequent history of Judaism was immeasurable. Its persistent character, and, it is not too much to say, the very preservation of its existence through all the vicissitudes of its fortunes, it owes more than anything else to the synagogue. Nor is it for Judaism alone that it had this importance. It determined the type of Christian worship, which in the Greek and Roman world of the day might otherwise easily have taken the form of a mere mystery; and, in part directly, in part through the church, it furnished the model to Mohammed. Thus Judaism gave to the world not only the fundamental ideas of these great monotheistic religions but the institutional forms in which they have perpetuated and propagated themselves.

George Foot Moore
Judaism in the First Centuries of the Christian Era

In the Synagogue All Are Spiritual Equals

What was originally and still remains largely unique in the worship of the synagogue is its thoroughly equalitarian structure. Not that individual Jewish congregations have never been oligarchically controlled, nor that the distinctions of wealth and social position which prevailed in the larger

Jewish community were always scrupulously kept out of the synagogue. The synagogue itself as an institution, however, has from its beginnings been firmly grounded on the principle of "the priesthood of all believers." In it there was no priestly hierarchy that could claim special religious authority, no dynastic order whose members were invested with unique privileges. Here all men were spiritual equals. Every man, even the humblest in station, could serve as the *sheliach tzibbur* or "emissary of the congregation" and lead it in worship, provided only that he was familiar with the prayers of the liturgy and the order of the service; and such familiarity, at least in times past, was the common property of virtually all Jews. The rabbi, who originally was not an official of the synagogue at all, was not regarded as endowed with any sacramental powers. He was merely a layman learned in the law, a teacher—as his title indicates—whose position derived solely from his scholarship and piety.

Bernard Martin
Prayer in Judaism

Any city that does not have these things, a scholar may not live there: A synagogue . . .

Sanhedrin 17b

The Values of Regular Public Worship

The individual, when he is his own standard, will pray when he feels he needs to. Prayer then, finds its occasion and its value in response to his private moods and feelings. What happens under those circumstances to regular prayer with respect to frequency, intensity, and unselfish content is a commonplace of modern versions of religiosity. The man who objects that he cannot pray on schedule often does not pray at all. And when, in this hectic world, he finally allows a conscious desire to pray to take priority over all the important things he should be doing now, he finds he does not have the knack. Obviously prayer in response to the inspiration of a moment has a unique significance, one well worthy of cherishing. But it is a supplement to, not a substitute for, regular public worship—and the acquired habit of turning to God in prayer is readily transferred from the congregational to the private situation.

Eugene B. Borowitz
Gates of Understanding

The Synagogue Is Basic

The synagogue must be recognized as the primary institution of Jewish life and affiliation. It, rather than any other type of corporate Jewish fellowship, fits into the American scene and it offers the only opportunity for making Judaism an enduring, living influence in American civilization. All other forms of activity and affiliation are helpful in that they advance one or another aspect of our collective being. But the synagogue is basic and fundamental. The synagogue is the most logical, the most American and the most all-embracing form of Jewish community expression. Remove the synagogue from the center of Jewish communal life and you reduce Jewishness, in the eyes of the Jewish community, to the lowest common denominator of racialism and lead our neighbors of other faiths to believe that we practice segregation to no purpose. Accentuate any secular type of Jewish fellowship as the essence of Jewishness and you inevitably court the inexorable fate of the American melting pot which fuses all secular groups into one. Make the synagogue the dynamic center of our collective being and the embassy of our spiritual life and you have a basis for permanent survival and for self-respecting relations with our fellow Americans. What other type of organization can offer such advantages and more fully guarantee our continued and unchallenged survival as American Jews?

Max Arzt
Address to Rabbinical Assembly of America, 1947

Jewish Worship Articulates Israel's Bond with God

Jewish worship is, classically, communal in character. Its Jewishness derives not from the external facts that Hebrew is used, traditional texts are recited, or Jewish symbols are displayed. It is Jewish because it is born out of the Covenant at Sinai and articulates Israel's bond with its God. The special language, texts, symbols all stem from this root relationship. Jewish worship, then, is the people of Israel, assembled before its God out of continuing loyalty to their Covenant, to acknowledge, praise, and petition Him. The group may be small; traditionally as few as ten are acceptable for a full public service. When at least ten Jews congregate to pray, they constitute the Covenant folk in miniature. They represent all Israel, past and present, here and everywhere. Not ten or more individuals, but the Covenant people itself now confronts its God. The man who prays in the synagogue prays as a participant in a Jewish history which continues into the living present, and his prayers, therefore, express the needs of the community in which he stands. Jewish law is clear. The individual Jew should seek to pray with a congregation. But if he cannot (that great phrase without which nothing could endure in history) then he may pray alone. Even alone, he should pray the congregational service (with some deletions), preferably at the time the congregation is praying. For a Jew, one's individuality is connected with being one *(sic!)* of the Jewish people, sharer in a mutual Covenant with God.

Eugene B. Borowitz
Gates of Understanding

A Community of Human Souls

Prayer is the most private of all human acts, needing to traverse intimate and emotionally vulnerable territory within the human self. At the same time, it is a universally shared human activity, one that surpasses all boundaries of language, culture, and even theology. To say it again in language influenced by Hasidism, prayer is the process by which the spark of divine light within each of us seeks out other sparks, the lights within all creation, and joins with them in the return to the one great source of light. In the course of this journey, the seeking out of those sparks that reside in other human souls, especially members of that soul family who speak the same religious language, becomes appropriate. For us Jews, prayer at its most profound and the communal activity of prayer should not be seen as conflicting with one another. Prayer in community should involve a reaching out to the soul of the other human and a joining together as a community of human souls together reaches toward God.

Arthur Green
The Reconstructionist

Prayer as a Means of Jewish Identification

Even though prayer is a personal experience because prayer affects the individual praying, the Jew prays as part of the Jewish community, as part of *K'lal Yisroel*. This is another reason why the prayers found in the prayer book are in the plural: "heal us," "save us," "forgive us," etc.

We can understand easily that our prayers are couched in the plural because "I am my brother's keeper" is a Jewish concept. How can we rest serenely, knowing that our fellow Jews are being persecuted in Russia? How can we have peace of mind knowing that our fellow Jews must ever be ready to give their lives in defense of the State of Israel? How can we remain silent when millions of human beings in underdeveloped countries all over the world are starving for lack of food? The least we can do to fulfill our obligation to these people is remember them in our prayers and, hopefully, these thoughts will stimulate us to action. It is these thoughts which the rabbis of the Talmud had in mind when they said, "whoever has it in his power to pray for his neighbor and fails to do so, is called a sinner."

By expressing this concern for the welfare of our fellow Jews in our prayers, we gain the understanding that there are bonds of unity which neither geographical distance nor Jewish denominational difference can break.

Tobias Roth
A Jewish View of Prayer and Worship

The Need for Experts

A Rabbi ordered his Warden to assemble ten men for a Minyan to chant Psalms for the recovery of a sick man. When they entered, a friend of the Rabbi exclaimed: "I see among them notorious thieves."

"Excellent," retorted the Rabbi. "When all the Heavenly Gates of Mercy are closed, it requires experts to open them."

Chasidic story

There is nothing sought by God except to hear the prayers of Israel.

Midrash Tehillim 116:1

9 GOD ALSO PRAYS

God Also Prays

The sages regarded prayer so important that they could even visualize the Almighty praying. Thus we find R. Johanan saying in the name of R. Jose: How do we know that the Holy One, blessed be He, says prayers? Because it says: "Even them will I bring to My holy mountain and make them joyful in My House of prayer" (Isaiah 56:7). It is not said, 'their house of prayer,' but 'My house of prayer'; hence you learn that the Holy one, blessed be He, says prayers.

Berachot 7a

God Is Both within Us and outside Us

Men once conceived of God as a king because in their experience the king had power over life and death and was the source of their blessings or curses. He could do anything and everything. So God became the King of kings. But this image is irrelevant in our day. The image of God as king is far from appealing. Perhaps we would be better served by the old Jewish idea of God as father. A father is both inside the child and outside him. He is, if you will, immanent and transcendent at one and the same time. In our childhood father was all-knowing, all-powerful; he could do everything. As we mature the image changes; father no longer knows everything and can do everything. Yet, he is probably closer and nearer to us, more meaningful and more necessary than when we were children. Analogies are always difficult, and even dangerous. A father is a human figure and God is not human. It is impossible to use language without falling into error when we try to picture God. Yet, if pictorialize we must, the figure of a father who loves us and cannot always do what he would love to do for us comes closer to our experience of God than that of an absolute monarch. A father needs his children and they need him. Modern men can more readily worship God viewed as father than as king.

Levi A. Olan
The Theological Foundations of Prayer

Sometimes

Sometimes God is seen, and sometimes He is not. Sometimes He listens, and sometimes not. Sometimes He can be sought, and sometimes not. Sometimes He can be found, and sometimes not. Sometimes He is near, and sometimes far.

Midrash Tanchuma, Ha'azinu 4

No One Is Closer than He

God appears far, but no one is closer than He. He is high above His universe, but a person can enter the synagogue, stand near the pulpit, and pray in a whisper—and God hears his prayer.

Yerushalmi, Berachot 9:1

The Pillars on Which Our Prayer Rises to God

It requires a great effort *to realize before Whom we stand*, for such realization is more than having a thought in one's mind. It is a knowledge in which the whole person is involved; the mind, the heart, body, and soul. To know it is to forget everything else, including the self. At best, we can only attain it for an instant, and only from time to time.

What then is left for us to do except *to pray for the ability to pray*, to bewail our ignorance of living in His presence? And even if such prayer is tainted with vanity, His mercy accepts and redeems our feeble efforts. It is the continuity of trying to pray, the unbroken loyalty to our duty to pray, that lends strength to our fragile worship; and it is the holiness of the community that bestows meaning upon our individual acts of worship. These are the three pillars on which our prayer rises to God: our own loyalty, the holiness of Israel, the mercy of God.

Abraham Joshua Heschel
God In Search of Man

God's Invitation to Live in His Presence

Judaism is God's invitation to man to live in the presence of the Almighty. Man may live in His presence because God desires him so to live. Man may seek God's closeness in prayer because God has made Himself known as the One who is close. Man may call on Him, because He desires to be called by man. "God is desirous of the prayers of Israel"; this is the foundation of the possibility of Jewish prayer. The Jew can pray because God has "opened his lips." Yehuda Halevi said of Judaism that it was begun by God, meaning that it was not a human discovery but a religion of revelation; it commenced with God's self-revelation. So is prayer in Judaism not the original creation of man but made possible by God who lets us come near by being near us. There is a temptation to compare revelation and prayer and to say that in revelation God addresses man, whereas in prayer man addresses God. One must overcome the temptation; it all begins with revelation. It is true that in revelation, God seeks man, and in prayer, man seeks God. However, man may seek God only because he knows that He may be found; and he knows that God may be found because he was first found by God.

Eliezer Berkovits
Studies in Torah Judaism

God Is Distant Yet Near

God is distant and yet near. How? R. Judah b. Simon said: From here (the earth) unto heaven is a journey of five hundred years; hence He is distant. Whence do we know that He is also near? A man stands at prayer and meditates in his heart and God is near unto his prayer, as it is said, "O Thou that hearest prayer, unto Thee doth all flesh come" (Psalm 65:3).

Midrash Deuteronomy Rabbah 2:10

Where God Dwells

Where does God dwell?

This was the question with which the Rabbi of Kotzk surprised a number of learned men who happened to be visiting him.

They laughed: "What a thing to ask! Is it not written, 'The whole world is full of his glory'?"

Then he answered his own question:

"God dwells wherever man lets him in."

Samuel H. Dresner
Prayer, Humility, and Compassion

God Always Accepts Us

It is written (Psalm 55:23), "Cast your burden upon God and He will sustain you." If a human being has a patron and he goes to him once, he accepts him. The second time, he accepts him. The third time, he does not appear to him. The fourth time, he does not even turn to him.

This is not true of God. For whenever you bother Him, He accepts you.

Midrash Tehillim 55:6

Even God prays. What is His prayer? "May it be My will that My love of compassion overwhelm My demand for strict justice."

Berachot 7a

The Dynamic of Ethical Action

The purpose in the various attempts to reinterpret the God idea is not to dissolve the God idea into ethics. It is to identify those experiences which should represent for us the actual working of what we understand by the conception of God. Without the actual awareness of His presence, experienced as beatitude and inner illumination, we are likely to be content with the humanistic interpretation of life. But this interpretation is inadequate, because it fails to express and to foster the feeling that man's ethical aspirations are part of a cosmic urge, by obeying which man makes himself at home in the universe. Without the emotional intuition of an inner harmony between human nature and universal nature, without the conviction, born of the heart rather than of the mind, that the world contains all that is necessary for human salvation, the assumptions necessary for ethical living remain cold hypotheses lacking all dynamic power. They are like an engine with all the parts intact and assembled, but lacking the fuel which alone can set it in operation. *The dynamic of ethical action is the spirit of worship, the feeling that we are in God and God in us*, the yielding of our persons in voluntary surrender to those larger aims that express for us as much as has been revealed to us of the destiny of the human race.

Mordecai M. Kaplan
The Meaning of God

Prayer—A Method of Cooperation with God

The idea of cooperation between man and God explains the significance of prayer. Apart from the dependence on God and the sense of reverence and worship of God's wisdom, power and holiness which it expresses, prayer is a method of cooperation with God in enabling man to meet a difficult situation. How God does His share man cannot presume to tell; but it is to the extent that we surrender ourselves in prayer, and attune our spirit to the spirit of God, that God responds to our calls upon Him, and meets us in our need.

Isidore Epstein
The Faith of Judaism

We Stand in Need of the God of Our Fathers

Pascal, one of the great mathematicians of history, sewed into the lining of the coat that he wore until the day of his death a scrap of paper upon which were written words that have a peculiar relevance today: "Not the God of the philosophers, but the God of Abraham, Isaac, and Jacob." Not the remote, aloof God of the philosophers—the concept or process, hypothesis or idea of which they speak—who cares little for man and his concerns, but the God of our fathers: the God who discovered Abraham in Ur of the Chaldees and tried him at Moriah, who appeared with a blessing in the night to Isaac at Beer-Sheba, who struggled in the darkness with Jacob in Beth El that he might be changed into Israel; the God who spoke of freedom to Moses at the burning bush, of holiness to Isaiah in the Temple of Jerusalem, of justice to Amos in the bleak wilderness near Tekoa, of judgment to Jeremiah and of forgiveness to Hosea; the God who struck awe into the heart of Job and love and fear into the soul of David, who taught Elijah to be afraid of no man and gave Nathan the strength to fight kings; who humbled Hillel and turned Akiba to repentance, who shone upon Maimonides, illumined Elijah of Vilna and set a ladder in the earth that the Baal Shem might ascend into heaven, the God who reveals His will, who hears our prayers, who shares our suffering, who has mercy on those in need and compassion for those in privation, who searches after righteous people and seeks out the upright man.

Pascal's phrase has a fiery meaning for our time, when many of us have been beguiled by the thinking of recent centuries which has attempted to remove God from the crucible of life and fit Him into the neat pages of a book, setting Him apart from the unavoidable decisions that confront us daily, the inescapable anxieties and worries, joys and comforts which are the lot of humankind, transforming Him into the objective and the debatable, the abstract and often irrelevant. We stand in need, not of the philosophers' God about which one reads in the cool of his study or speculates upon in the leisure of the lecture hall, who is distant and unconcerned, remote and unapproachable; but of our fathers' God who pursues us "down the nights and down the days . . . down the arches of the years," seeking to enter our hearts and souls and lives.

Samuel H. Dresner
Prayer, Humility, and Compassion

Praying to God as Process

I know that it is very hard for people who have been in the habit of thinking of God as a person, to understand how one can address God if one regards God as a cosmic process. I don't think that it is so difficult if you understand that as being really is—I am talking to you, are you just static entities? Isn't everyone of you a life, and isn't life a process? Are you to whom I am talking the same being that you were on the day you were born? Are you not constantly becoming something different? You are a process and I am talking to you. I can talk in the same way and with the same freedom with that cosmic process which I regard as the very source and fountain of my own being.

Eugene Kohn
Good to Be a Jew

God—The Distant He and the Nearby Thou

The prayers of Judaism say, "I am his, and he is mine." For Judaism God is not only the distant He, but is also the nearby Thou to whom its prayers are addressed. In this joint vision is apprehended the unity of the God of remoteness and the God of immediacy. That is why the Bible uses the two words, He and Thou, interchangeably, even in the same sentence. "He" and "thou" follow immediately upon one another. "The Lord is a high tower for the oppressed, a high tower in times of trouble, and they that know Thy name put their trust in Thee: for Thou, Lord hast not forsaken them that seek Thee" (Psalm 9:10f.). "He shall cover thee with His pinions and under His wings shalt thou take refuge; His truth is a shield and a buckler. . . . Because thou hast said, The Lord is my refuge, and hast made the most High thy habitation" (Psalm 91:4f.). "It is a good thing to give thanks unto the Lord and to sing praises unto Thy name, O most High" (Psalm 92:2). "Return unto thy rest, O my soul; for the Lord hath dealt bountifully with thee. For Thou hast delivered my soul from death, mine eyes from tears, and my feet from falling" (Psalm 116:7f.). Again and again this shift from "he" to "thou" and from "thou" to "he." In these waves of emotion there is a reiterated approaching and grasping, a seeking and attracting by which the "he" always becomes "thou."

Leo Baeck
The Essence of Judaism

Simon the Pious said: In his prayer a man should think that the Shechinah is before him.

Sanhedrin 22a

The Beckoning God Wants Us to Grow

Once a disciple said to a Chasidic Rabbi, "Master, why is it that God sometimes seems so far away?" The Rabbi replied, "Imagine a father teaching a child to walk. He does not hold on to the child. On the contrary, he holds his arms outstretched away from the child, and the child walks forward, in between the arms. As the child comes forward, the father moves further away. How else is the child to learn to walk?"

All is not a bed of roses for us on this earth, because were it otherwise, we would never develop into our humanity. We would never rise towards God. God is near with His outstretched arms, but He does not want us to remain infantile. He wants us to develop our divinity. And as we go forward (seemingly alone), we come closer to God. As we develop our faculties for independent thinking and loving and sharing, we approach reality in life; but each time we come forward, the "Father" recedes, the goal becomes higher as we ascend another rung, the vision of God grows in scope as we ascend the ladder of spirituality. Once we have God wrapped up in a nice pretty package-definition stuffed away in our pocket or in a bank vault, we may know that we have a false vision. A God, too well defined, who serves as a crutch at all times, who keeps us in the dependent infantile state, is no God at all, but a projection of a childish wish. A mature projection of God (and God is not dependent upon our projection of Him) will picture God in the image of a beckoning God who urges us to grow towards Him in love and understanding.

This dramatic image of the Chasidic Rabbi teaches us that God beckons us onward in order that we might develop our potential powers. The Chasidim called this "redeeming oneself." As we walk forward, drawn by God, we become less dependent on Him; that is, we learn how to fend for ourselves in this world. *The person who prays seeks ways to become independent*; as he grows towards God, he becomes able to deal with life's problems without despairing and without becoming over-anxious or fearful.

It was Jeremiah who prophesied the time when men would not have to teach one another about God because each man would have the knowledge of God in his heart. The man who goes in search of God regularly (who prays) becomes less dependent (i.e., fulfills his potential as a man) because he learns what God wants him to know. The developed man communes easily and regularly with God "in his heart" and is sensitive to the nearness of God. He lives and moves in the prayer-state.

Philo, the great Jewish philosopher, who lived in Egypt in the 1st century, wrote, "*He who flees from God, flees into himself.*" We can apply this insight here. If going towards God means the development of one's better self, then one "who flees from God" is he who regresses, i.e., he settles for what he is, he "flees *into* himself" (as he is—not what he might be). The prayer-mood is a conscious attempt to improve oneself by the contemplation of a greatness towards which one would like to grow. Thus, our pursuit (imitation) of God is, in a healthy way, a flight from oneself (i.e., from the stagnating self). Prayer is the search for one's higher self, one's real self.

Martin Buber
Tales of the Hasidim
quoted by Herbert M. Baumgard in
Judaism and Prayer

Before God All Are Equal

R. Judah b. Shalom said in the name of R. Eleazar: If a rich man speaks, immediately he is heard and listened to. Before God, however, all are equal, women, slaves, poor and rich. A proof? Because of Moses, the greatest of all prophets, the same is said as of a poor man. Of Moses it is written, "A prayer of Moses the man of God" (Psalm 90:1), and of a poor man it says, "A Prayer of the poor, when he fainteth, and poureth out his complaint before the Lord" (Psalm 102:1). In both cases the word "prayer" is used to teach you that before God all are equal in prayer.

Exodus Rabbah 21:4

God's Holiness—Fortress of the Oppressed

"Thou art Holy, Thy Name is Holy. . . . Praised be Thou O God of Holiness."

The holiness of God, the supreme statement of the moral nature of the Divine, is a basic concept in Judaism and has an important bearing on the whole conception of prayer. God's holiness, which means God's supreme ethical perfection, implies that to Him the ill-used may confidently turn for justice and the persecuted for mercy. Among no pagan nation whose gods were pictured as pleasure-loving, mutually jealous and brutal, could prayer ever rise to so noble a height.

It is only the consciousness that the Universe is dominated by a Holy God, by a justice without flaw, a mercy without stint, a goodness without limit, which can give to the heart-broken, and the forlorn one final court of appeal. God's holiness is the last fortress of the persecuted and the oppressed.

This concept of the Divine Holiness, without which the unfortunate would be left bereft of hope forever, received further development in the Prayerbook. The holiness of God became the sun to which every human soul like an earth-born plant raises itself to flower and fruit. God's holiness is not merely a splendor, distant and unattainable, but a light, absorbed and reflected and sought for in every human life. This was already expressed in the Bible (Leviticus 19:2), "Ye shall be holy; for I the Lord your God am holy."

Solomon B. Freehof
The Small Sanctuary

ACKNOWLEDGMENTS

The author gratefully acknowledges the following publishers and authors for their kind permission to use excerpts from the following books:

Man's Quest For God by Abraham Joshua Heschel, reprinted by permission of Charles Scribner's Sons, an imprint of Macmillan Publishing Company. Copyright 1954 Abraham Joshua Heschel; copyright renewed © 1982 Hannah Susannah Heschel and Sylvia Heschel.

Gates of Understanding edited by Laurence A. Hoffman, including passages by Eugene B. Borowitz, Henry Slonimsky, Roland B. Gittelsohn, and Laurence A. Hoffman, reprinted by permission of Union of American Hebrew Congregations.

Hidden Hungers by Sidney Greenberg, reprinted by permission of Hartmore House.

Prayer, Humility, and Compassion by Samuel H. Dresner, reprinted by permission of Hartmore House.

Levi Yitzchak of Berditchev by Samuel H. Dresner, reprinted by permission of Hartmore House.

Likrat Shabbat by Sidney Greenberg and Jonathan Levine, reprinted by permission of Prayer Book Press.

Passages from the 1959 "Judaism" by Eliezer Berkovitz and the 1961 Summer "Judaism" by Steven Schwarzchild. Reprinted by permission of the American Jewish Congress. Copyrights 1959, 1961 American Jewish Congress.

Prayer in Judaism by Bernard Martin, reprinted by permission of Basic Books.

This Is My God by Herman Wouk, reprinted by permission of the author.

The Traditional Prayer Book by David De Sola Pool, reprinted by permission of Behrman House Books.

Guideposts in Modern Judaism by Jacob B. Agus, *A Faith for Moderns* by Robert Gordis, and *Daily Prayer Book* by Joseph H. Hertz are reprinted by permission of Bloch Publishing Company.

Tradition and Contemporary Experience edited by Alfred Jospe, including a portion of "On the Meaning of Prayer" by Ernst Simon, reprinted by permission of B'nai B'rith Hillel Foundations.

Passages by Jeremy Silver from *CCAR Journal* 1965, and portions of the 1967 CCAR *Proceedings* by Jakob J. Petuchowski, reprinted by permission of the Central Conference of American Rabbis.

"Modernizing the Jewish Prayer Book" by T. H. Gaster reprinted from *Commentary*, April 1954. By permission; all rights reserved.

Nineteen Letters by Samson Raphael Hirsch, reprinted by permission of Feldheim Publishers.

Man's Best Hope by Roland B. Gittelsohn, reprinted by permission of the author.

Jewish Philosophy and Pattern of Life by Simon Greenberg, reprinted by permission of the author.

Studies in Torah Judaism: Prayer by Eliezer Berkovits, reprinted by permission of Yeshiva University.

Basic Judaism by Milton Steinberg, copyright 1947 by Milton Steinberg, renewed by David Joel Steinberg and Jonathan Steinberg. Reprinted by permission of Harcourt Brace Jovanovich, Inc.

The Efficacy of Prayer by Dudley Weinberg, reprinted by permission of the Jewish Chautauqua Society.

Jewish Prayer by Louis Jacobs, reprinted by permission of Jewish Chronicle Publications.

Jewish Worship by Abraham Millgram, reprinted by permission of the Jewish Publication Society of America. Copyright © 1971 by the Jewish Publication Society.

The Synagogue in Jewish Life by Joshua Cohen, reprinted by permission of Ktav Publishing House, Inc.

Understanding Jewish Prayer by Jakob J. Petuchowski, reprinted by permission of Ktav Publishing House, Inc. and the author.

A Living Covenant by David Hartmann, reprinted by permission of The Free Press, a Division of Macmillan Inc. Copyright © 1985 by The Free Press.

Sabbath and Festival Prayer Book by Simon Greenberg and Louis Finkelstein, reprinted by permission of The Rabbinical Assembly. Copyright © 1946, 1973 by The Rabbinical Assembly and the United Synagogue of America.

Address from the *Proceedings* of The Rabbinical Assembly 1947 by Max Arzt, reprinted by permission of The Rabbinical Assembly. Copyright 1948 by The Rabbinical Assembly.

The World of Sholem Aleichem by Maurice Samuel, reprinted by permission of Alfred A. Knopf.

The Meaning of God In Jewish Life, Religion, and *Questions Jews Ask* by Mordecai M. Kaplan, reprinted by permission of Reconstructionist Press.

Meditations on the Siddur by B. S. Jacobson, reprinted by permission of Sinai Bookstore and Publishing Company.

Prayer by Abraham Kon, reprinted by permission of Soncino Press Ltd.

Judaism and Prayer by Herbert M. Baumgard, *The Theological Foundation of Prayer,* edited by Jack Bemgrad, and *The Small Sanctuary* by Solomon B. Freehof, reprinted by permission of Union of American Hebrew Congregations.

The Jewish Way of Life by Rabbi David Aronson, reprinted by permission of United Synagogue of America.

Your Word Is Fire: The Hasidic Masters on Contemplative Prayer translated and edited by Arthur Green and Barry Holtz, reprinted by permission of Arthur Green.

AUTHOR INDEX